ACIDS, BASES AND SALTS

◈ Atlantic Europe Publishing

First published in 1998 by Atlantic Europe Publishing
Company Limited, Greys Court Farm, Greys Court,
Henley-on-Thames, Oxon, RG9 4PG, UK.

**Copyright © 1998
Atlantic Europe Publishing Company Limited**

Author
Brian Knapp, BSc, PhD
Project consultant
*Keith B. Walshaw, MA, BSc, DPhil
(Head of Chemistry, Leighton Park School)*
Project Director
Duncan McCrae, BSc
Editor
Mary Sanders, BSc
Special photography
Ian Gledhill
Illustrations
The Ascenders Partnership, David Woodroffe
Designed and produced by
EARTHSCAPE EDITIONS
Print consultants
Chromo Litho Ltd
Reproduced in Malaysia by
Global Colour
Printed and bound in Italy by
L.E.G.O. SpA

Suggested cataloguing location
Knapp, Brian
  Acids, Bases and Salts
  ISBN 1 869860 42 X
  – ChemLab series, volume 5
540

Picture credits
All photographs are from the **Earthscape
Editions** photolibrary except the
following:
(c=centre t=top b=bottom l=left r=right)
ICI(UK) 9cr; **Mary Evans Picture
Library** 6tr, 7tr, 8cl, 8tr

*This product is manufactured from sustainable
managed forests. For every tree cut down at
least one more is planted.*

Contents

HOW TO USE THIS BOOK
These two pages show you how to get the most from this book.

❶ THE CONTENTS

Use the table of contents to see how this book is divided into themes. Each theme may have one or more demonstrations.

❷ THEMES

Each theme begins with a theory section on yellow-coloured paper. Major themes may contain several pages of theory for the demonstrations that are presented on the subsequent pages. They also contain biographies of scientists, whose work was important in the understanding of the theme.

❸ DEMONSTRATIONS

Demonstrations are at the heart of any chemistry study. However, many demonstrations cannot easily be shown to a whole class for health and safety reasons, because the demonstration requires a close-up view, because it is over too quickly, takes too long to complete, or because it requires special apparatus. The demonstrations shown here have been photographed especially to overcome these problems and give you a very close-up view of the key stages in each reaction.

The text, pictures and diagrams are closely connected. To get the best from the demonstration, look closely at each picture as soon as its reference occurs in the text.

Many of the pictures show enlarged views of parts of the demonstration to help you see exactly what is happening. Notice, too, that most pictures form part of a sequence. You will find that it pays to look at the picture sequence more than once, and always be careful to make sure you can see exactly what is described in any picture before you move on.

The main heading for a demonstration or a set of demonstrations.

An introduction expands on the heading, summarising the demonstration or group of demonstrations and their context in the theme.

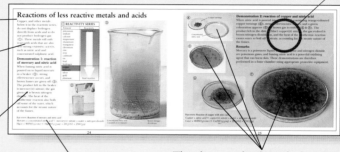

Each demonstration is carefully explained and illustrated with photographs and, where necessary, with diagrams, tables and graphs. The illustrations referred to are numbered ①, ②, ③, etc.

Chemical equations are shown where appropriate (see the explanation of equations at the bottom of page 5).

The photographs show the key stages that you might see if you witness a demonstration at first-hand. Examine them very carefully against the text description.

APPARATUS

The demonstrations have been carefully conducted as representative examples of the main chemical processes. The apparatus used is standard, but other choices are possible and you may see different equipment in your laboratory, so make sure you understand the principles behind the apparatus selected. The key pieces of apparatus are defined in the glossary.

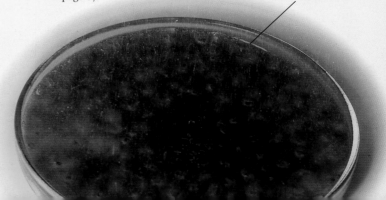

❹ GLOSSARY OF TECHNICAL TERMS

Words with which you may be unfamiliar are shown in small capitals where they first occur in the text. Use the glossary on pages 66–74 to find more information about these technical words. Over 400 items are presented alphabetically.

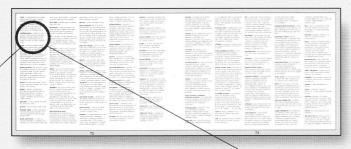

❺ INDEX TO ALL VOLUMES IN THE SET

To look for key words in any of the 12 volumes that make up the ChemLab set, use the Master Index on pages 75 to 80. The instructions on page 75 show you how to cross-reference between volumes.

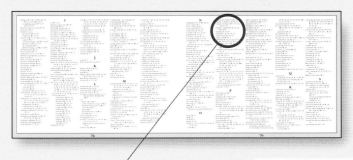

The most important locations of the term 'oxidising agent' are given in a master index which includes references to all of the volumes in the ChemLab set.

oxidising agent: a substance that removes electrons from another substance being oxidised (and therefore is itself reduced) in a redox reaction. *Example:* chlorine (Cl_2).

ABBREVIATIONS

Units are in the international metric system. Some units of measurement are abbreviated, or shortened, as follows:
°C = degrees Celsius
km = kilometre
m = metre
cm = centimetre
mm = millimetre
sq m = square metre
g = gram
kg = kilogram
kJ = kilojoule
l = litre

❻ CHEMICAL EQUATIONS

Important or relevant chemical equations are shown in written and symbolic form together with additional information.

What the reaction equation illustrates

Where relevant, the oxidation state is shown as Roman numerals in brackets.

Word equation

Symbol equation
The symbols for each element can be found in any Periodic Table.

EQUATION: Reaction of copper and nitric acid
Copper + nitric acid ⇨ *copper(II) nitrate + water + nitrogen dioxide*
$Cu(s) + 4HNO_3(conc) ⇨ Cu(NO_3)_2(aq) + 2H_2O(l) + 2NO_2(g)$
Blue

The symbol indicating the state of each substance is shown as follows:
(s) = solid
(g) = gaseous
(l) = liquid
(aq) = aqueous
($conc$) = concentrated

The two halves of the chemical equation are separated by the arrow that shows the progression of the reaction. Each side of the equation must balance.

Sometimes additional descriptions are given below the symbol equation.

The correct number of atoms, ions and molecules and their proportions in any compound are shown by the numbers. A free electron is shown as an e^-.

ACIDS

Acids are one of the fundamental groups of substances in chemistry and have fascinated chemists for thousands of years. Acids were first noticed as natural products of fermentation. It was discovered, for example, that if grapes fermented for too long they produced a sour-tasting liquid, vinegar, instead of wine. This is why the word 'acid' comes from the Latin for sour, 'acidus'.

The scientific investigation of acids thus began with naturally occurring acids. It was found that, if the vinegar was boiled and the vapours collected, then a pure acid (now called ethanoic acid, CH_3COOH) could be obtained. Such acids are called ORGANIC ACIDS and contain carbon, oxygen and hydrogen in their formula. Many other acids were also extracted from animal and plant materials.

Organic acids were not easy to work with. The other main group of acids (now called MINERAL ACIDS because they were derived from rock materials, or minerals) was discovered later. Nitric acid, for example, was discovered in the 8th century and sulphuric acid was discovered in the 10th century. However, they proved to be easier to use.

The first people to use mineral acids (in particular hydrochloric acid (HCl), nitric acid (HNO_3) and sulphuric acid (H_2SO_4)) were physicians trying to develop medicines, and ALCHEMISTS (medieval experimenters who wanted to turn lead into gold).

Mineral acids are more reactive than organic acids. As a result, mineral acids are called STRONG ACIDS and organic acids are described as WEAK ACIDS.

Over the centuries that followed, experimenters were especially interested in 'royal water' or 'aqua regia'. This was the alchemists' name for a mixture of nitric acid and hydrochloric acid which supposedly could 'dissolve' gold.

How acids work

One of the major challenges in chemistry has been to find out how acids work. Three centuries ago, scientists

GREAT EXPERIMENTAL SCIENTISTS
Antoine Laurent Lavoisier

Antoine Laurent Lavoisier (1743–1794) was born in Paris, the son of a prosperous lawyer. He was interested in geology, and to learn about minerals he attended chemistry classes.

Lavoisier has been called the 'father of chemistry'. His insistence on the need to make careful measurements was particularly valuable, and from this came the recognition that the weight of the reactants must equal the weight of the products of a reaction. This helped the development of a logical theory which could pull all the parts of chemistry together.

Lavoisier thought that there must be a substance which all acids had in common. He thought this (wrongly as it turned out) to be oxygen. It was from this mistaken belief that he coined the name oxygen, which means 'acid-producing'.

Lavoisier was caught up in the French Revolution, and he was imprisoned and finally guillotined based on trumped-up charges. At the time a fellow scientists remarked: "It took only an instant to cut off that head, and a hundred years may not produce another like it."

had already grasped the notion that chemicals were made of enormous numbers of tiny, similar particles. In the 17th century, the French scientist Betrand, suggested that acids were sour because they were made of tiny particles that had spikes that pricked the tongue. Bases (oxides and hydroxides of METALS) he thought to be made of particles with holes, so that, when acids and bases came together, the spikes fitted into the holes and cancelled each other out. The result was NEUTRALISATION.

In the 18th century, the French scientist Antoine Lavoisier looked for a fundamental link shared by all acids, and which gave them their special properties. Lavoisier thought that this was the ELEMENT oxygen. However, although many acids do contain oxygen, some do not.

By the 19th century, experimentation led British scientist Sir Humphry Davy and the French scientists Joseph L. Gay-Lussac and Louis J. Thénard to show that the common link was hydrogen rather than oxygen. With this sure foundation, the German chemist Justus von Liebig was able to define an acid as a COMPOUND that contains hydrogen in a form that can be replaced by a metal.

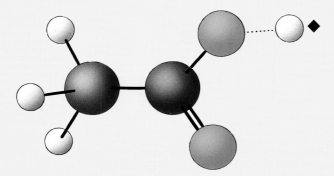

(Above) This is a representation of ethanoic acid, also known as acetic acid (CH₃COOH), which is found in vinegar. The hydrogen atom marked with the "◆" symbol will dissociate from the molecule when in water. This is what makes this compound an acid.

GREAT EXPERIMENTAL SCIENTISTS
Sir Humphry Davy

Sir Humphry Davy (1778–1829) was a famous English chemist born in Cornwall. He was the first to discover many metals, including sodium and potassium. He was also one of the first to make extensive studies in electrochemistry. His experiments supported the theory that acids dissociate in water and that they contain hydrogen.

Davy was educated as an apothecary and had to train himself in science. He was fascinated by the ideas of another famous scientist, Lavoisier, and he began to experiment with light and heat. In 1801 he was asked to become lecturer on chemistry at the Royal Institution of Great Britain in London, which had just been founded. In the following years, Davy made some remarkable discoveries and also was a very popular lecturer.

Just a year before Davy was made lecturer in chemistry, Alessandro Volta made the world's first battery. This was used to dissociate water into oxygen and hydrogen, a process called ELECTROLYSIS.

Davy was eager to agree with Lavoisier that acids contain oxygen, but in 1810 he performed sufficient experiments on hydrochloric acid to convince himself that it was actually hydrogen that was the common element. Davy went on to OXIDISE hydrochloric acid and in doing so, discovered that, when oxygen combined with the hydrogen in the acid, it released a hitherto unknown element. Davy was thus the first person to discover the element chlorine.

Nevertheless, this did not prove to be the end to the search for the true nature of an acid. By 1887, the Swedish chemist, Svante Arrhenius, proposed a more complete theory to account for acid behaviour. This is now called the ionic theory.

The ionic theory of Arrhenius suggests that, when an acid is placed in water it ionises – is converted into small charged particles, or IONS.

An acid releases hydrogen ions, $H^+(aq)$. So, for example, nitric acid (HNO_3) in water yields H^+ and NO_3^- (nitrate) ions, sulphuric acid in water yields H^+ and SO_4^{2-} (sulphate) ions, and hydrochloric acid in water yields H^+ and Cl^- (chloride) ions.

The ionic theory is very important because it shows that, although there are many substances containing hydrogen, if they do not release hydrogen ions when placed in a solution, they cannot behave as acids. Thus, for example, methane (CH_4) is a substance that contains hydrogen but which does not ionise and so is not an acid.

More recently, the ionic theory of Arrhenius has been improved further by a Danish chemist, Johannes Brönsted, and a British chemist, T. M. Lowry. They produced the theory that an acid is a substance that can donate a PROTON to another substance.

MANUFACTURING AN ACID

Mineral acids are produced industrially by reacting a suitable gas with water. Here, the example of sulphuric acid is shown, which involves the reaction of sulphur trioxide gas with water. This is known as the Contact Process.

The steps involved are shown below.

1. Burning of sulphur in air to produce sulphur dioxide gas. Molten sulphur is pumped into a combustion furnace together with a blast of dry air. The resultant mixture of gases includes impurities, which are removed by trickling the gas through previously produced concentrated sulphuric acid.

2. The most efficient way of causing sulphur dioxide and oxygen to combine to yield sulphur trioxide (SO_3) is to heat them together at 400°C. However, this is too slow a process for industrial use and so a variety of temperatures and a CATALYST of vanadium(V) oxide are used to speed up the process in the converter.

3. The sulphur trioxide gas enters a tower which has a mist of sulphuric acid sprayed into it. The sulphur trioxide is absorbed into the acid, forming fuming sulphuric acid (called 'oleum', $H_2S_2O_7$) which is 99.5% pure acid.

Water is added to the fuming sulphuric acid to obtain the acid concentration required commercially.

EQUATION: Stage 1: Obtaining sulphur dioxide from sulphur

Sulphur + oxygen ⇨ sulphur dioxide

$S(l) + O_2(g) ⇨ SO_2(g)$

EQUATION: Stage 2: Reacting sulphur dioxide and oxygen to produce sulphur trioxide

Sulphur dioxide + oxygen ⇨ sulphur trioxide

$2SO_2(g) + O_2(g) ⇨ 2SO_3(g)$

EQUATION: Stage 3: Overall reaction – water with dissolved sulphur trioxide to form concentrated sulphuric acid

Sulphur trioxide + water ⇨ concentrated sulphuric acid

$SO_3(g)$ (absorbed in H_2SO_4) + $H_2O(l) ⇨ H_2SO_4(conc)$

(Right) **A bank of Contact Process converters.**

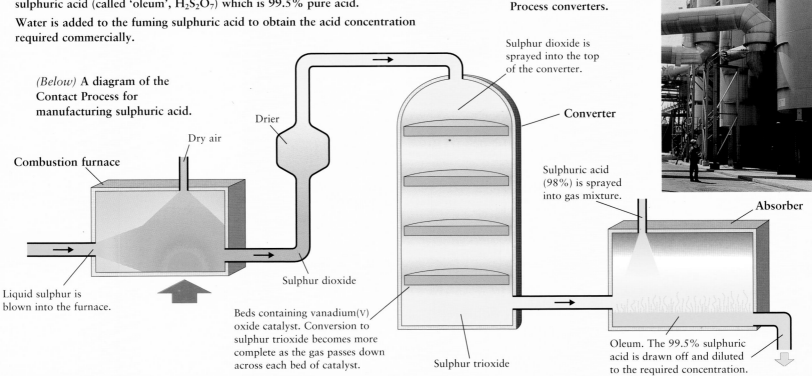

(Below) **A diagram of the Contact Process for manufacturing sulphuric acid.**

Drier

Dry air

Combustion furnace

Liquid sulphur is blown into the furnace.

Sulphur dioxide

Beds containing vanadium(V) oxide catalyst. Conversion to sulphur trioxide becomes more complete as the gas passes down across each bed of catalyst.

Sulphur trioxide

Sulphur dioxide is sprayed into the top of the converter.

Converter

Sulphuric acid (98%) is sprayed into gas mixture.

Absorber

Oleum. The 99.5% sulphuric acid is drawn off and diluted to the required concentration.

Chemical reactions that are typical of acids

There are several typical reactions that all acids share:

(i) Acids react with the more reactive metals, such as magnesium and zinc, to release hydrogen gas (① and pages 11 to 14).

(ii) Acids react with metal oxides and hydroxides (bases) to form salts and water (page 16).

(iii) Acids react with carbonates to release carbon dioxide and produce a salt and water (pages 18 to 23).

(iv) When aqueous solutions of acids are electrolysed, hydrogen is given off at the negative electrode (page 26).

(v) Acids neutralise bases (page 42 and 55 to 61).

(vi) Acids cause certain substances, called indicators, to change colour. For example, blue litmus is turned red by acids (page 64).

Notice that, together, these properties can also be used as tests for an acid, although usually the use of an indicator is sufficient.

How acids react with metals

Metals (on the left of the PERIODIC TABLE) have 1, 2 or even 3 more ELECTRONS than they need for stability. If they react with an acid, they give up these electrons and become positively charged ions. For these metals to react, the electrons they give up must be accepted by some other chemical. Hydrogen ions produced by acids in water can readily accept electrons. Each hydrogen ion accepts an electron and becomes a hydrogen ATOM. Pairs of hydrogen atoms then form hydrogen molecules which are given off as hydrogen gas. The metal then combines with the remaining ions (such as the chloride ions if the acid was hydrochloric acid) to form a salt.

THE REACTIVITY SERIES		
Element	Reactivity	Reaction with metals
Potassium Sodium Calcium Magnesium Aluminium Manganese Chromium Zinc Iron Cadmium Tin Lead	*Most reactive* Increasing reactivity	*More reactive metals: Hydrogen gas is released on reaction with an acid.*
Hydrogen		
Copper Mercury Silver Gold Platinum	*Least reactive*	*Less reactive metals: No hydrogen gas will be released. Only acids that are also oxidising agents will react with these metals.*

(Above) The position of the metal relative to hydrogen in the activity series tells us whether the metal can produce hydrogen gas when reacted with an acid. Those above hydrogen in the series will reduce hydrogen ions in the acid to hydrogen and liberate hydrogen gas. Those below hydrogen in the table will not.

Potassium and sodium react dangerously fast with acids. Metals which react at a safe rate include those below sodium in the table.

Acids and reactive metals

The reaction of a metal with an acid depends on the reactivity of the metal. As shown on page 10, metals can be placed in order of their reactivity – the reactivity series – with the most reactive at the top, and the least reactive at the bottom. Hydrogen can also be placed in this scale. This is important because hydrogen can only be released from an acid–metal reaction of the metal if the metal is above hydrogen in the REACTIVITY SERIES.

If the metal is below hydrogen, then no hydrogen will be released. For example, if copper is placed in a beaker and some hydrochloric acid is added, no reaction will occur, and no gas will be given off.

Demonstration 1: testing that a metal–acid reaction produces hydrogen

Zinc is above hydrogen in the reactivity series and so when reacted with an acid it will produce hydrogen. In this demonstration, dilute hydrochloric acid from a dropper funnel is reacted with zinc granules in a conical flask (①).

As the metal and the acid react, heat is given off, and there is effervescence (②, page 12). The gas produced is taken through a delivery tube and collected in a gas jar over water in a pneumatic trough (③).

When the gas jar is filled with gas, it is lifted out of the water, and the mouth of the jar is sealed with a glass cover slip (hydrogen is lighter than air). The gas can then be tested.

① Dilute hydrochloric acid is poured into the dropper funnel and released carefully on to the zinc metal.

The hydrogen gas that is evolved is collected in a gas jar over water.

Zinc

EQUATION: Zinc and dilute hydrochloric acid
Hydrochloric acid + zinc ⇨ hydrogen + zinc chloride
$2HCl(aq) + Zn(s) ⇨ H_2(g) + ZnCl_2(aq)$
ACID + METAL ⇨ HYDROGEN GAS + SALT

When a long, lighted splint (④) is put into an inverted gas jar containing hydrogen, a small explosion occurs at the mouth of the jar where the hydrogen and air mix. This is heard as a loud, high-pitched, 'popping' sound.

The splint goes out where it is entirely within the hydrogen (⑤), but it relights some way down its length at the point where the hydrogen and air are mixing and COMBUSTING (⑥).

The effervescence is caused by hydrogen gas bubbles released during the reaction.

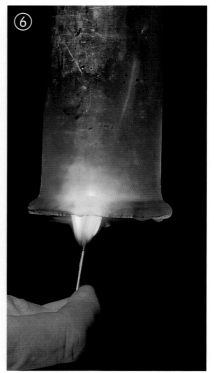

Demonstration 2: reaction of dilute hydrochloric acid and magnesium

When a piece of magnesium ribbon (which has been scraped clean to remove the oxide layer) is dropped into a beaker containing dilute hydrochloric acid (⑦) the reaction is much more vigorous than with zinc (⑧). Magnesium is more reactive than zinc and not only is the hydrogen produced more rapidly but heat is produced more rapidly too. This can be seen as steamy fumes.

EQUATION: Magnesium and hydrochloric acid

Magnesium + hydrochloric acid ⇨ hydrogen + magnesium chloride

$Mg(s) + 2HCl(aq) ⇨ H_2(g) + MgCl_2(aq)$

ACID + METAL ⇨ HYDROGEN GAS + SALT

⑧

⑦

Magnesium ribbon cleaned with emery paper

Bubbles of hydrogen gas

Dilute hydrochloric acid

Demonstration 3: dilute sulphuric acid and zinc

The use of sulphuric acid in place of hydrochloric acid also yields hydrogen gas with reactive metals. In the simple demonstration shown here, dilute sulphuric acid is added to a beaker containing a piece of sheet zinc (⑨). During the reaction, hydrogen gas is given off which can be seen as effervescence on the surface of the zinc (⑩).

If this reaction is conducted in apparatus similar to that shown on page 11, the gas can be collected and tested for hydrogen.

Dilute hydrochloric acid

Cut zinc strip

Bubbles of hydrogen gas

EQUATION: Zinc and sulphuric acid
Zinc + sulphuric acid ⇨ hydrogen + water + zinc sulphate
$Zn(s) + H_2SO_4(aq) ⇨ H_2(g) + ZnSO_4(s)$
ACID + METAL ⇨ HYDROGEN GAS + SALT

Acids and less reactive metals

Those metals below hydrogen in the reactivity series will not react with an acid to produce hydrogen gas. Only acids that are powerful OXIDISING AGENTS will react with these less reactive metals. Nitric acid and concentrated sulphuric acid are both powerful oxidising agents.

Demonstration: nitric acid and copper

When concentrated nitric acid (which is yellow) is poured on to copper turnings in a side-arm boiling tube, vigorous effervescence occurs and a green–blue colouration appears in the liquid at the bottom of the boiling tube (①). The blue colouration comes from the copper ions in the copper nitrate that is produced by the reaction. A brown gas is also evolved that is nitrogen dioxide, and the heat of the EXOTHERMIC reaction causes water to boil off, accounting for the steamy nature of the fumes.

The only other reddish-brown gas is bromine. To distinguish between the two gases, wetted green pH paper is placed in the gas. The pH paper is turned a bright red by the acidic gas, but is bleached more slowly by nitrogen dioxide than it would be for bromine (②).

Remarks

Nitrogen dioxide is a poisonous gas, and fuming nitric acid is a powerful oxidising agent that can harm skin. This demonstration is therefore performed in a fume chamber.

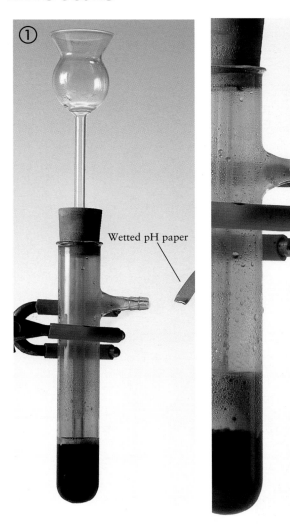

Wetted pH paper

EQUATION: Copper and nitric acid
Copper + nitric acid ⇨ nitrogen dioxide + copper nitrate + water
$Cu(s) + 4HNO_3(conc) ⇨ 2NO_2(g) + Cu(NO_3)_2(s) + 2H_2O(l)$
Blue

Acids and oxides or hydroxides

Acids react with oxides or hydroxides of metals (see pages 42 and 49 for more on bases and salts) to produce a salt of that metal and water only.

Unlike the reaction of acids with pure metal, the oxygen present in a metal oxide reacts with the hydrogen in the acid to form water, and so hydrogen is not released.

Demonstration: reaction of dilute sulphuric acid and copper(II) oxide

If dilute sulphuric acid (colourless) is poured on to a small pile of black copper(II) oxide powder in a beaker (①), the oxygen in the oxide reacts with the acid to produce a blue copper(II) sulphate solution and water (②). No effervescence occurs, as no gas is formed.

Copper(II) oxide

Dilute sulphuric acid

Glass stirring rod

Copper(II) sulphate

EQUATION: Reaction of dilute sulphuric acid and copper(II) oxide
Sulphuric acid + copper(II) oxide ⇨ copper(II) sulphate + water
$H_2SO_4(aq) + CuO(s) \Rightarrow CuSO_4(aq) + H_2O(aq)$
ACID + BASE ⇨ SALT + WATER

16

Acids and nitrates

In general, acids do not react with metal nitrates. One exception is concentrated sulphuric acid, which will react with potassium nitrate to produce fuming nitric acid.

Demonstration: reaction of concentrated sulphuric acid with potassium nitrate

The reaction between concentrated sulphuric acid and potassium nitrate produces fuming nitric acid, which is highly corrosive. For this reason, the apparatus consists entirely of glassware, and no rubber or plastic stoppers are used.

Some potassium nitrate is placed in the bowl of a retort. The neck from the retort leads into a long-necked, round-bottomed flask in a cold-water bath. The water bath causes the vapour formed during the demonstration to condense.

Some concentrated sulphuric acid is poured over the potassium nitrate (①) and a glass stopper is fitted. Brown fumes of nitrogen dioxide are formed, together with oxygen and water vapour (②). However, most of the vapour distilling is nitric acid vapour, which condenses to liquid in the cooled flask. Some nitrogen dioxide dissolves in this liquid, turning it yellow.

Remarks

This is a demonstration of the preparation of a strong acid. For the preparation of a weak acid, see page 34.

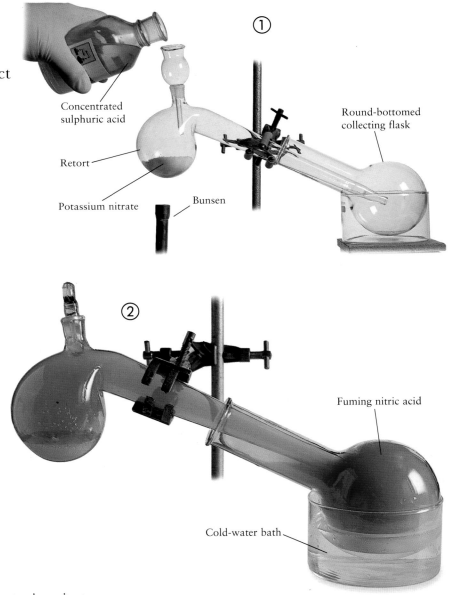

Concentrated sulphuric acid

Retort

Potassium nitrate

Bunsen

①

Round-bottomed collecting flask

②

Fuming nitric acid

Cold-water bath

EQUATION: Reaction of concentrated sulphuric acid and potassium nitrate
Concentrated sulphuric acid + potassium nitrate ⇨ fuming nitric acid + potassium hydrogen sulphate
$H_2SO_4(conc) + KNO_3(s) \Rightarrow HNO_3(g) + KHSO_4(s)$

Acids and carbonates

All carbonates will react with mineral acids to release carbon dioxide gas.

Demonstration 1: reaction of an acid with calcium carbonate and sodium hydrogen carbonate

Dilute mineral acids will react with any carbonate of a metal to release carbon dioxide gas.

In this demonstration, some marble (calcium carbonate) chips are placed in the bottom of a long-necked, flat-bottomed flask (①). Dilute hydrochloric acid is added, and effervescence of carbon dioxide begins immediately (②). The foam produced rises up into the neck of the flask (③).

If the reaction is conducted in a side-arm boiling tube, the gas can be tested by passing it through colourless limewater (calcium hydroxide) (④ & ⑤). The cloudiness that develops as the gas bubbles through the limewater is a positive test for carbon dioxide (⑥).

EQUATION: Dilute hydrochloric acid with calcium carbonate
Dilute hydrochloric acid + calcium carbonate ⇨ calcium chloride + carbon dioxide + water
$2HCl(aq) + CaCO_3(s) ⇨ CO_2(g) + CaCl_2(aq) + H_2O(l)$
ACID + CARBONATE ⇨ CARBON DIOXIDE + SALT + WATER

①

Calcium carbonate chips

②

Dilute hydrochloric acid

Carbon dioxide gas

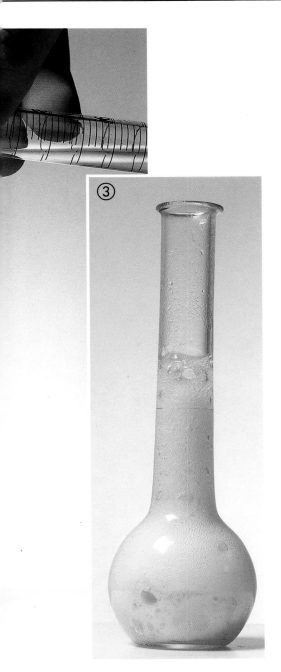

Limewater

Demonstration 2: reaction of an acid with sodium hydrogen carbonate

As with carbonates, acids react with hydrogen carbonates (bicarbonates) to produce carbon dioxide and water.

In this simple demonstration, sodium hydrogen carbonate in the form of an antacid tablet is held in dilute hydrochloric acid with a pair of metal tongs and effervescence of carbon dioxide begins immediately (⑦). (Stomach acid contains dilute hydrochloric acid.)

EQUATION 2: Reaction of dilute hydrochloric acid with sodium bicarbonate
Dilute hydrochloric acid + sodium bicarbonate ⇨ carbon dioxide + sodium chloride + water
$HCl(aq) + NaHCO_3(s) \Rightarrow CO_2(g) + NaCl(aq) + H_2O(l)$
ACID + CARBONATE ⇨ CARBON DIOXIDE + SALT + WATER

Demonstration 3: reaction of an acid with copper carbonate

If dilute sulphuric acid is added to green copper carbonate crystals in a conical flask (⑧), effervescence immediately takes place and carbon dioxide gas is given off (⑨).

The effervescence churns up the copper carbonate powder as it reacts with, and dissolves in, the acid, making the liquid appear muddy (⑩). The mixture finally clears to produce a blue solution of copper(II) sulphate (see page 16).

The rate of reaction depends on the strength and concentration of the acid.

EQUATION: Reaction of dilute sulphuric acid and copper carbonate

Sulphuric acid + copper carbonate ⇨ carbon dioxide + copper sulphate + water

$$H_2SO_4(aq) + CuCO_3(s) \Rightarrow CO_2(g) + CuSO_4(aq) + H_2O(l)$$

ACID + CARBONATE ⇨ CARBON DIOXIDE + SALT + WATER

⑩

⑧

Dilute sulphuric acid

Copper carbonate

⑨

Carbon dioxide gas

Acids and sulphites, sulphides and nitrites

As with carbonates, acids will react with sulphites, sulphides and nitrites to release a gas. Acids do not react with sulphates.

Demonstration 1: reaction of an acid with a sulphide

Hydrogen sulphide is a very poisonous gas, and so should be prepared in a fume chamber, even when prepared in small quantities.

In this demonstration, some sodium sulphide powder is first put into a test tube. Dilute hydrochloric acid is then added slowly using a pipette (①). No external source of heating is required.

As the acid and the sodium sulphide react, a vigorous bubbling occurs and a colourless solution of sodium chloride forms (②). The gas can be tested by passing it over filter paper soaked in colourless lead nitrate. Hydrogen sulphide turns the lead nitrate solution dark brown (③). This is a standard laboratory test for a sulphide.

Dilute hydrochloric acid

Sodium sulphide

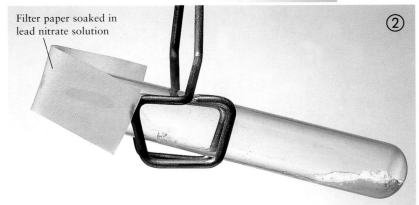

Filter paper soaked in lead nitrate solution

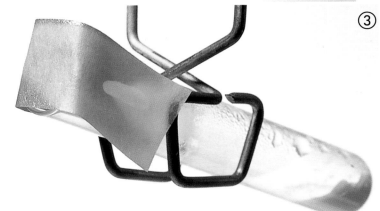

EQUATION: Dilute hydrochloric acid with sodium sulphide

Hydrochloric acid + sodium sulphide ⇨ hydrogen sulphide + sodium chloride

$2HCl(aq) + Na_2S(s) \Rightarrow H_2S(g) + 2NaCl(aq)$

ACID + SULPHIDE ⇨ GAS + SALT

Demonstration 2: reaction of an acid with a sulphite

Sodium sulphite (a white powder) is first placed in the test tube and some dilute hydrochloric acid is then added through a pipette. The reaction will take place without any external source of heating and sulphur dioxide gas is produced.

As with hydrogen sulphide, sulphur dioxide is a poisonous gas and so should be prepared in a fume chamber, even when prepared in small quantities.

Sulphur dioxide is extremely soluble in water, and much of the first gas produced will therefore be absorbed into the solution of reactants. Thus it may be some while before effervescence is observed.

To test for sulphur dioxide gas, a piece of filter paper soaked in orange potassium dichromate solution is placed over the mouth of the test tube (④). Sulphur dioxide is a strong reducing agent and will change the potassium dichromate solution to a blue–green colour, which may appear almost white on the filter paper (⑤). This is the standard preparation of sulphur dioxide gas in the laboratory, and a standard test for a sulphite.

Demonstration 3: reaction of an acid with a nitrite

Dilute sulphuric acid is added to a white powder of sodium nitrite (⑥) and colourless nitrogen monoxide is produced. This reacts rapidly with the oxygen in the air near the mouth of the test tube (⑦) to form clearly visible brown nitrogen dioxide gas (⑧). Nitrogen monoxide and nitrogen dioxide are very poisonous, and so this test is done in a fume chamber.

Remarks

Carbonates, sulphites, sulphides and nitrites are known as weak ACID RADICALS.

EQUATION: Dilute hydrochloric acid with sodium sulphite
Dilute hydrochloric acid + sodium sulphite ⇨ sulphur dioxide + sodium chloride + water
$2HCl(aq) + Na_2SO_3(s) ⇨ SO_2(g) + 2NaCl(aq) + H_2O(l)$
ACID + SULPHITE ⇨ GAS + SALT + WATER

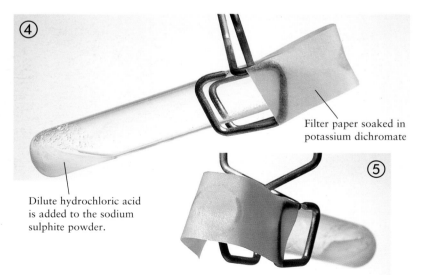

④

⑤

Filter paper soaked in potassium dichromate

Dilute hydrochloric acid is added to the sodium sulphite powder.

EQUATION: Dilute sulphuric acid with sodium nitrite
Dilute sulphuric acid + sodium nitrite ⇨ sodium sulphate + nitric acid
+ nitrogen monoxide + water
$3H_2SO_4(aq) + 6NaNO_2(s) ⇨ 3Na_2SO_4(s) + 2HNO_3(aq) + 4NO(g) + 2H_2O(l)$

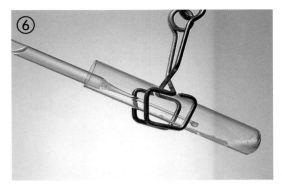

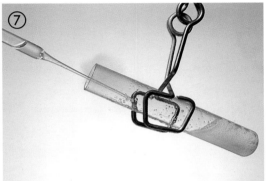

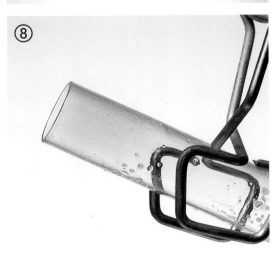

Concentrated sulphuric acid and chlorides

The reaction of concentrated sulphuric acid with a metal chloride produces the dangerous gas, hydrogen chloride.

Demonstration: reaction of concentrated sulphuric acid with hydrogen chloride

The most common chloride is sodium chloride, the main component of common salt.

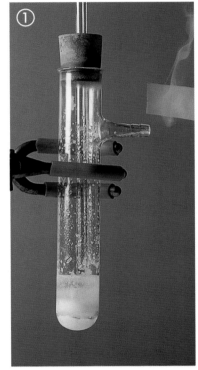

In this demonstration, some white sodium chloride powder is placed in a side-arm boiling tube, and some concentrated sulphuric acid is added through a thistle funnel. The reaction produces considerable effervescence and does not need external heating. The sulphuric acid displaces the hydrogen chloride as a gas. Because hydrogen chloride gas is corrosive, this demonstration is done in a fume chamber.

The presence of hydrogen chloride gas can be verified by dipping a piece of filter paper in ammonia solution and placing this in the flow of gas (①). If hydrogen chloride is present, it will create a white smoke of ammonium chloride.

EQUATION: Dilute sulphuric acid and sodium chloride
Dilute sulphuric acid + sodium chloride ⇨ hydrogen chloride gas + sodium hydrogen sulphate
$H_2SO_4(aq) + NaCl(s) ⇨ HCl(g) + NaHSO_4(aq)$
ACID + CHLORIDE ⇨ HYDROGEN CHLORIDE GAS + SALT

Acids as oxidising agents

Two of the three main mineral acids commonly used in the laboratory – concentrated sulphuric acid and concentrated nitric acid – are powerful oxidising agents that are used to react with the less reactive metals. In many situations, the acid will be a stronger oxidising agent than the substance it is reacting with. The third main mineral acid, hydrochloric acid, does not behave as an oxidising agent.

Demonstration 1: nitric acid as an oxidising agent

Concentrated nitric acid will even react with mercury, one of the more unreactive metals (see page 10).

When fuming nitric acid is poured on to liquid mercury in a beaker (①), vigorous effervescence occurs, and brown fumes of nitrogen dioxide are given off (②). The product left in the beaker is mercury(II) nitrate.

Demonstration 2: hydrochloric acid as a reducing agent

When hydrochloric acid is oxidised, chlorine is displaced from the acid. This is a standard preparation for chlorine gas.

In this demonstration, purple crystals of potassium permanganate (a powerful oxidising agent) are placed in a flask. Concentrated hydrochloric acid is dripped on to the potassium permanganate crystals, using a dropper funnel.

①

Fuming nitric acid is poured on to mercury.

Mercury

EQUATION: Reaction of mercury and nitric acid
Mercury + concentrated nitric acid ⇨ mercury(II) nitrate + water + nitrogen dioxide
$Hg(s) + 4HNO_3(conc) ⇨ Hg(NO_3)_2(aq) + 2H_2O(l) + 2NO_2(g)$

②

A green-coloured gas immediately begins to fill the flask and is collected in a gas jar (③). Chlorine is the only common green gas.

The hydrochloric acid has been oxidised to chlorine and water.

Remarks

Chlorine is poisonous and so this reaction must be conducted in a fume chamber.

Brown nitrogen dioxide gas

③

EQUATION: Reaction of hydrochloric acid with potassium permanganate
Concentrated hydrochloric acid + potassium permanganate ⇨ chlorine + water + manganese(II) chloride + potassium chloride
$16HCl(conc) + 2KMnO_4(s) ⇨ 5Cl_2(g) + 8H_2O(l) + 2MnCl_2(aq) + 2KCl(aq)$

Demonstration 3: reaction of alcohol (cyclohexanol) with concentrated nitric acid

Concentrated nitric acid will also oxidise many organic compounds, such as ALCOHOLS.

This demonstration is performed in a tall gas jar, inside a fume chamber. A very small volume of (colourless) cyclohexanol is first poured into one measuring cylinder and (colourless) concentrated nitric acid into the other cylinder (④). It is very important to notice that only small volumes of starting reactants are being used here. Large amounts could produce a reaction of dangerously violent proportions.

The gas jar contains a stirring thermometer, which will show the amount of heat given out during the demonstration.

The cyclohexanol is poured into the gas jar (⑤), followed by the nitric acid (⑥). All of the nitric acid is added as quickly as possible because the reaction is almost instantly violent, and hands need to be clear of the apparatus by the time the reaction starts (⑦).

The reaction immediately produces a 'volcanic' eruption of bubbling liquid and a gush of brown gas (nitrogen dioxide) (⑧ & ⑨). As the bubbling subsides and the gas clears, the temperature of the thermometer is found to have risen from 20°C to 110°C (⑩).

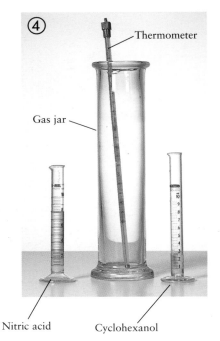

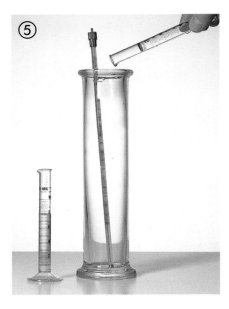

EQUATION: The oxidation of cyclohexanol
Cyclohexanol + concentrated nitric acid ⇨ *nitrogen dioxide + hexandioic acid + water*
$C_6H_{11}OH(l) + 8HNO_3(conc)$ ⇨ $8NO_2(g) + (CH_2)_4(CO_2H)_2(l) + 5H_2O(l)$
Heat given out

Acids as electrolytes

Pure water is not a good ELECTROLYTE. But, when an acid is dissolved in water it ionises, forming a solution that will conduct electricity. An acid electrolyte can be broken up by electrolysis, and hydrogen will be released from the solution at the negative electrode.

Demonstration: electrolysis of dilute sulphuric acid

In this laboratory demonstration, a side-arm U-tube is fitted with two ELECTRODES made of platinum. Each electrode passes through a stopper and is connected to a Direct Current (DC) power pack. In this case, the negative electrode is on the left and the positive electrode on the right.

The U-tube is filled with dilute sulphuric acid until the levels are a little way below the side arms. Each side arm is connected to a delivery tube which, in turn, leads under

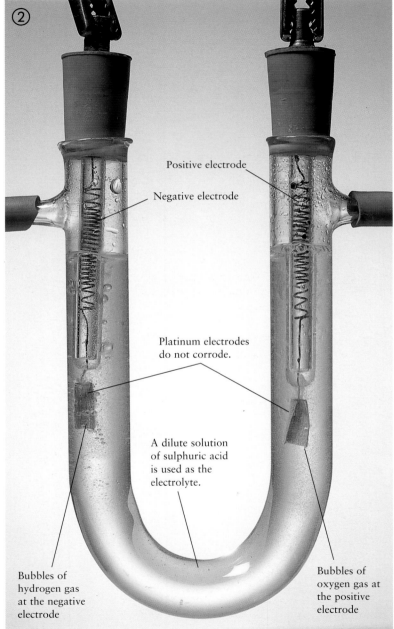

Positive electrode

Negative electrode

Platinum electrodes do not corrode.

A dilute solution of sulphuric acid is used as the electrolyte.

Bubbles of hydrogen gas at the negative electrode

Bubbles of oxygen gas at the positive electrode

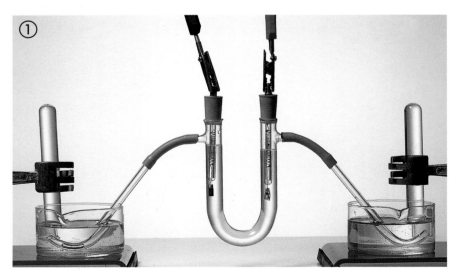

an upturned boiling tube filled with water and supported in a pneumatic trough (①). The purpose of this system is to collect gases produced during electrolysis.

As soon as the power supply is switched on, the ions in the acid solution are attracted to the electrodes (②). When the ions reach the electrodes, some either lose or take up electrons. Hydrogen ions (H^+), which are positively charged ions, migrate to the negative electrode and form molecules of hydrogen gas (H_2). This gas is collected in the left-hand tube (③).

The negative hydroxide ions (OH^-) and sulphate ions (SO_4^{2-}) migrate to the positive electrode. The hydroxide ions contribute oxygen atoms, which combine to form molecules of oxygen gas (O_2), which is collected in the right-hand boiling tube.

The hydrogen gas can be tested for using a lighted splint. A loud, high-pitched 'popping' sound can be heard if the splint is brought to the mouth of the tube when lifted from the water. The oxygen, on the other hand, will rekindle a glowing splint.

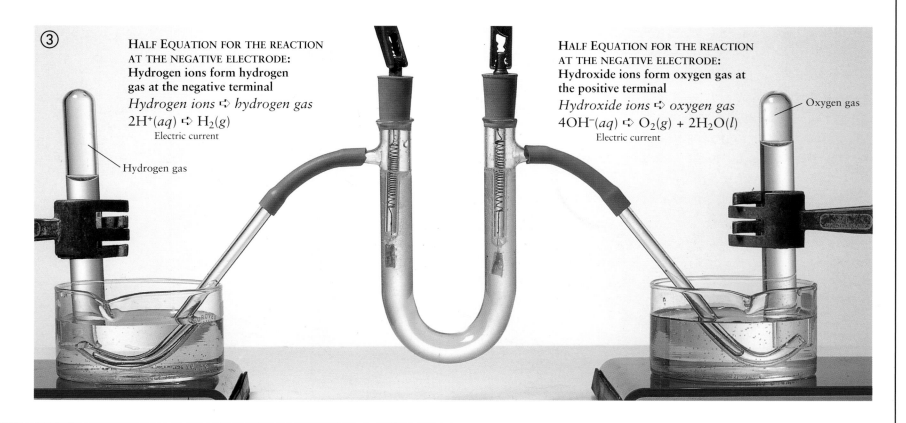

③

HALF EQUATION FOR THE REACTION AT THE NEGATIVE ELECTRODE:
Hydrogen ions form hydrogen gas at the negative terminal
Hydrogen ions ⇨ hydrogen gas
$2H^+(aq) ⇨ H_2(g)$
Electric current

Hydrogen gas

HALF EQUATION FOR THE REACTION AT THE NEGATIVE ELECTRODE:
Hydroxide ions form oxygen gas at the positive terminal
Hydroxide ions ⇨ oxygen gas
$4OH^-(aq) ⇨ O_2(g) + 2H_2O(l)$
Electric current

Oxygen gas

The importance of water in acids

Any substance that has acidic properties will ionise. That is, it will form ions when dissolved in water. The test for acidic properties is therefore to test whether there are hydrogen ions in the solution.

Demonstration 1: a solution of hydrogen chloride gas in methylbenzene has no acidic properties

In the next two demonstrations, hydrogen chloride gas is bubbled through two liquids, methylbenzene and then water. The resulting solutions are then tested for their acidic properties.

Hydrogen chloride gas is prepared by reacting sodium chloride with dilute sulphuric acid in a conical flask. The gas is taken through a delivery tube and some flexible rubber tubing, and released through a funnel. The funnel allows the gas to spread out over a large surface area to maximise the opportunities for the gas to dissolve (①).

In this first demonstration, some methylbenzene is poured into a beaker (②).

Hydrogen chloride gas contains no ions. If it is dissolved in methylbenzene, the result is hydrogen chloride molecules mixed in with methylbenzene molecules. There are no hydrogen (H^+) ions and there can be no acidity.

In fact, hydrogen chloride readily escapes from the methylbenzene and so, after some time, almost as many bubbles of gas are seen rising out of the methylbenzene as can be seen bubbling in the generating flask (③). The escaping hydrogen chloride gas can be detected by placing a filter paper soaked in ammonia over the beaker (④). The hydrogen chloride fumes interact with the ammonia,

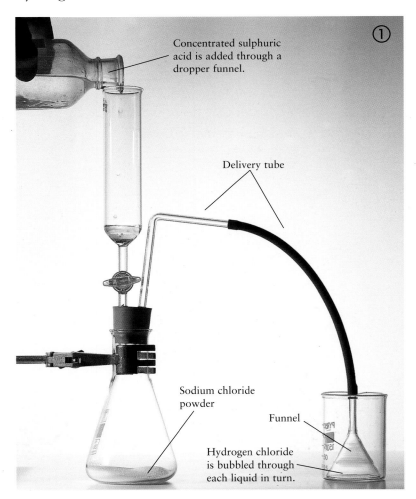

① Concentrated sulphuric acid is added through a dropper funnel.

Delivery tube

Sodium chloride powder

Funnel

Hydrogen chloride is bubbled through each liquid in turn.

and a dense smoke (of white ammonium chloride particles) is produced.

Two test tubes are now made up with the dry (no water) liquid methylbenzene containing the hydrogen chloride gas. They are both colourless. A piece of magnesium ribbon is placed in one (⑤), and anhydrous sodium carbonate is placed in the other (⑥).

No reaction occurs either in the tube with the magnesium or with the sodium carbonate, showing that hydrogen chloride gas cannot behave as an acid when not in water. To prove that hydrogen chloride is still present, a piece of filter paper is soaked in ammonia and placed over the neck of the tube. This still produces white smoke (⑦, page 32).

④ Ammonium chloride smoke

Filter paper soaked in ammonia solution

These two test tubes contain a dry methylbenzene solution of hydrogen chloride.

⑤   ⑥

Magnesium ribbon does not react.

Anhydrous sodium carbonate does not react.

② Methylbenzene

③

Filter paper soaked in ammonia solution

⑦

Demonstration 2: a solution of hydrogen chloride in water has acidic properties

The demonstration is repeated with water as the liquid in the beaker (⑧). Hydrogen chloride is very soluble in water and so, although vigorous bubbling occurs in the flask generating hydrogen chloride gas, little bubbling can be seen in the beaker (⑨). The hydrogen chloride gas is dissolving as fast as it is being produced and thus is forming an aqueous (in water) solution of hydrogen chloride, in other words, it is hydrochloric acid.

Two more test tubes are set up containing the aqueous solution, and a piece of magnesium ribbon is placed in one (⑩), and some anhydrous sodium carbonate placed in the other (⑪). Vigorous reactions occur in both test tubes. At the end of these reactions, the sodium carbonate and the magnesium ribbon have been entirely used up, showing that there was an excess of acid in the tubes. The two tubes containing methylbenzene remain with unreacted reagents in them.

Remarks

Without the presence of water, there is nothing in the methylbenzene solution to stabilise the hydrogen ion. This is because the hydrogen ion is really a hydroxonium (or hydronium) ion (H_3O^+), and a water molecule is required to stabilise it.

It is the presence of ions that allows acids to act as an electrolyte and undergo electrolysis. And, it is the presence of a high concentration of hydrogen ions that gives strong acids their common properties.

Distilled water

These two test tubes contain a dry methylbenzene solution of hydrogen chloride.

These two test tubes contain an aqueous solution of hydrogen chloride.

Magnesium ribbon remains unreacted.

Anhydrous sodium carbonate remains unreacted.

Magnesium ribbon reacts.

Anhydrous sodium carbonate reacts.

Distinguishing between strong and weak acids

Mineral acids ionise much more readily than organic acids. An acid that has ionised almost completely is called a strong acid, whereas an acid that is poorly ionised is called a weak acid. Because an ionised solution is a good conductor of electricity (it is a good electrolyte), a strong acid should have a good CONDUCTIVITY, whereas a weak acid should have a low conductivity.

Demonstration: comparing the conductivity of sulphuric acid and ethanoic acid

The apparatus consists of a specially shaped glass container (a conductivity cell) containing a pair of electrodes. The electrodes consist of two small platinum discs mounted a fixed distance apart (①).

To compare the conductivity of these acids, the conductivity cell is connected to a laboratory power pack and an ammeter.

Two solutions of acid have to be prepared so that they have the same concentration, that is, they both contain an equal number of molecules of acid which could ionise.

One of the acids is then poured into the conductivity cell, the power pack is switched on, and the electrical current passing through the solution is immediately read from the ammeter (②). The acid is then poured away and the cell thoroughly rinsed out with distilled water. The second acid is now poured into the conductivity cell and the reading noted (③). In this demonstration, the reading given by the sulphuric acid is 0.8 amp, whereas

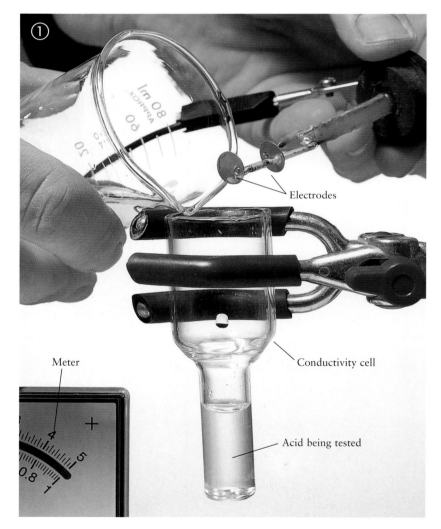

Electrodes

Conductivity cell

Acid being tested

Meter

the reading given by the ethanoic acid is 0.05 amp. The conductivity of the sulphuric acid is far higher than the conductivity of the ethanoic acid, showing that sulphuric acid is the stronger acid.

Remarks

If a Direct Current (DC) supply is used, as in this case, the readings must be taken as soon as the circuit is completed and before bubbles have formed on the electrodes.

An Alternating Current (AC) supply could be used instead to prevent electrolysis occurring and forming gases on the electrodes. The presence of non-conducting gases can reduce the conducting area on the electrode and thus give distorted and non-comparable results. (The use of AC also prevents the corrosion of one of the electrodes and so ensures a longer life for the apparatus.)

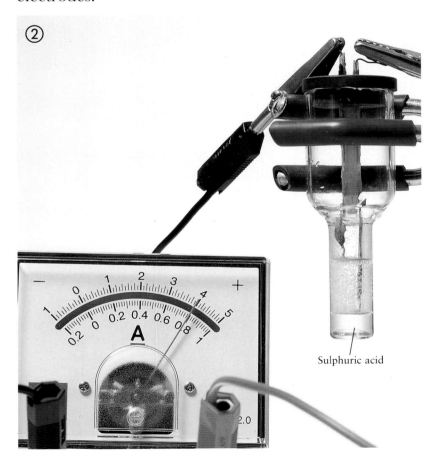

Sulphuric acid

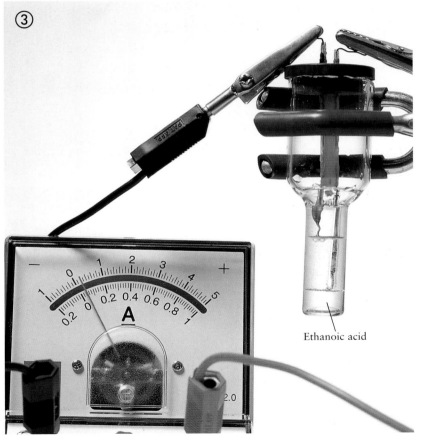

Ethanoic acid

Formation of a weak acid

Carbonic acid is a weak organic acid. It can be produced by passing carbon dioxide through distilled water.

Demonstration: preparation of carbonic acid

In this demonstration, a continuous flow of carbon dioxide gas is required. This is most easily prepared by using a Kipp's apparatus (①). The delivery tube from the Kipp's apparatus is taken to a gas jar which contains tap water and a few drops of Universal Indicator, so that we can readily see the changes taking place (②).

At the start of the demonstration, the solution is blue because the tap water used is slightly alkaline; but, as carbon dioxide bubbles through, the colour changes quickly to a strong green (③), then to a yellowy-green (④), then yellow (⑤), and finally pink (⑥). It does not turn red even if carbon dioxide is bubbled through for a long time. The pink, rather than red, colour of the indicator shows that the solution is a weak acid (a high concentration of hydrogen ions is never produced).

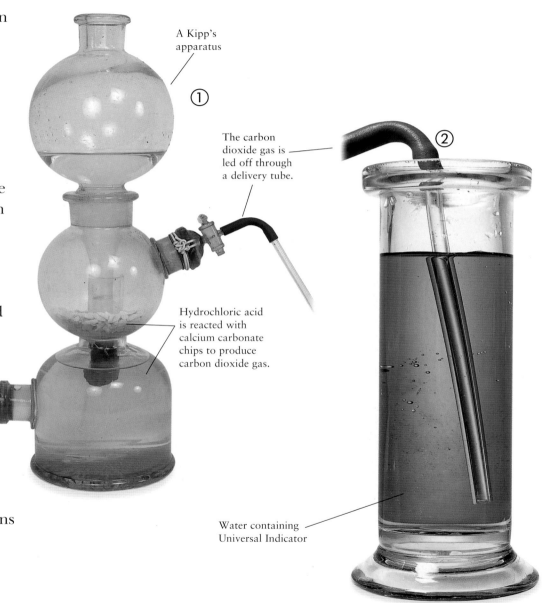

A Kipp's apparatus ①

The carbon dioxide gas is led off through a delivery tube.

②

Hydrochloric acid is reacted with calcium carbonate chips to produce carbon dioxide gas.

Water containing Universal Indicator

Remarks

Carbonic acid is a weak acid, produced naturally as a result of the interaction of carbon dioxide in the air and water droplets in clouds. This is the acid that is primarily responsible for the sculpting of limestone landscapes, worldwide. All organic acids are weak acids. Other examples include citric acid (in the juice of citrus plants) and ethanoic acid (in vinegar).

EQUATION: **Reaction of carbon dioxide and water**
Carbon dioxide + water ⇨ carbonic acid
$CO_2(g) + H_2O(l) ⇨ H_2CO_3(aq)$

Bubbles of carbon dioxide

Concentrated sulphuric acid as a dehydrating agent

A DEHYDRATING AGENT is a substance that removes water from another substance. Sulphuric acid is also a powerful drying agent.

Demonstration 1: drying properties of concentrated sulphuric acid

Concentrated sulphuric acid has a strong affinity for water and will absorb it from the air to make a more dilute solution of the acid, becoming progressively more HYDRATED. This can be used to show the presence of water vapour in the air because, over time, the volume of very concentrated sulphuric acid exposed to air will increase as it absorbs water.

To demonstrate this property, two bottles, one half filled with water and the other containing an equal volume of concentrated sulphuric acid (yellow dye was added to identify the acid), are placed inside an airtight container (①). Over the following weeks, the concentrated sulphuric acid takes the water out of (dries) the air and becomes more dilute. Evaporation occurs from the bottle containing the water, and this water vapour is also absorbed by the concentrated acid. As a result, the level of liquid in the acid bottle rises and the acid becomes more dilute, while the level in the water bottle falls (②).

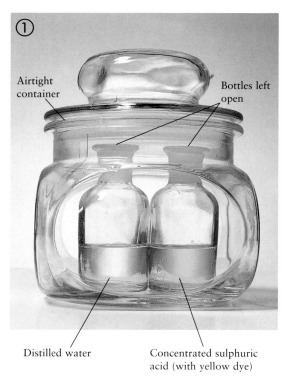

Distilled water

Concentrated sulphuric acid (with yellow dye)

Evaporation of water

Hydration of sulphuric acid

Demonstration 2: dehydration of copper(II) sulphate using concentrated sulphuric acid

A disc of dark blue, hydrated copper(II) sulphate crystals is prepared by allowing some copper(II) sulphate solution to evaporate in a Petri dish. Hydrated copper(II) sulphate is more accurately named

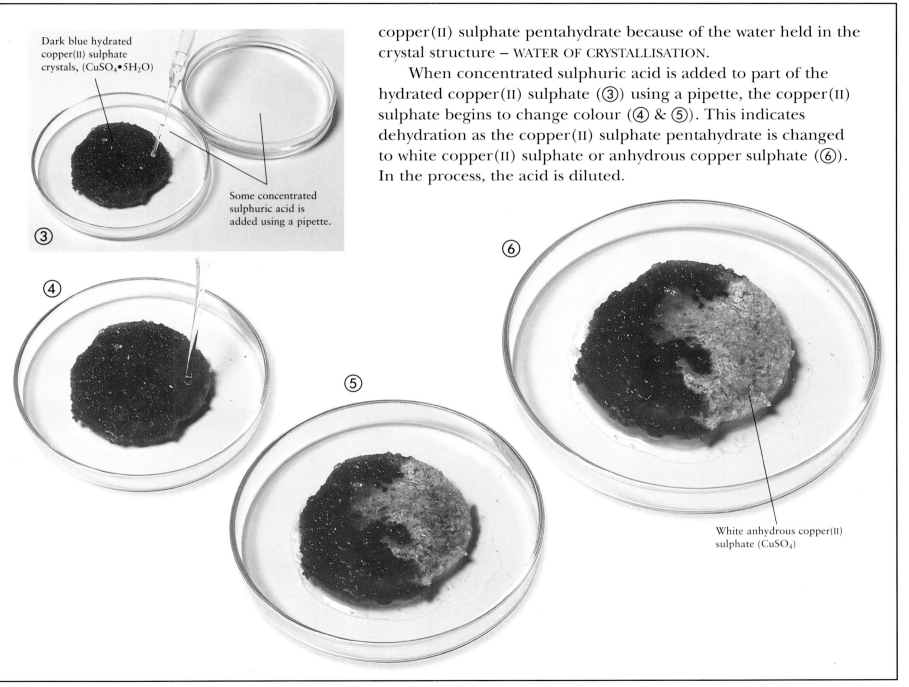

Dark blue hydrated copper(II) sulphate crystals, ($CuSO_4 \cdot 5H_2O$)

Some concentrated sulphuric acid is added using a pipette.

③

④

⑤

⑥

White anhydrous copper(II) sulphate ($CuSO_4$)

copper(II) sulphate pentahydrate because of the water held in the crystal structure – WATER OF CRYSTALLISATION.

When concentrated sulphuric acid is added to part of the hydrated copper(II) sulphate (③) using a pipette, the copper(II) sulphate begins to change colour (④ & ⑤). This indicates dehydration as the copper(II) sulphate pentahydrate is changed to white copper(II) sulphate or anhydrous copper sulphate (⑥). In the process, the acid is diluted.

Demonstration 3: dehydration of sucrose using concentrated sulphuric acid

Hot, concentrated sulphuric acid can remove water from many compounds. In this demonstration, some sugar (sucrose) is placed in a boiling tube and concentrated sulphuric acid is added (①). The sugar becomes liquid, turning first yellow (②), then brown (③) and finally black. After a minute or so, the surface of the liquid bulges up and cracks. By now, so much heat is given out that much of the surplus water produced by the dehydration reaction forms steam. The steam bubbles are trapped in the sticky, black carbon creating a froth that rises up the tube (④ & ⑤). When the reaction is over, and the heat subsides, the frothed carbon sets hard (⑥).

Remarks

If sulphuric acid touches human skin, the molecules in the skin immediately begin to lose their water (dehydrate). This effect is commonly known as acid burn.

Acid burns are among the most serious accidents that can happen in the laboratory, especially if splashes should get into the eye. This is the main reason why protective glasses should be worn at all times when handling mineral acids, especially those with oxidising and dehydrating properties.

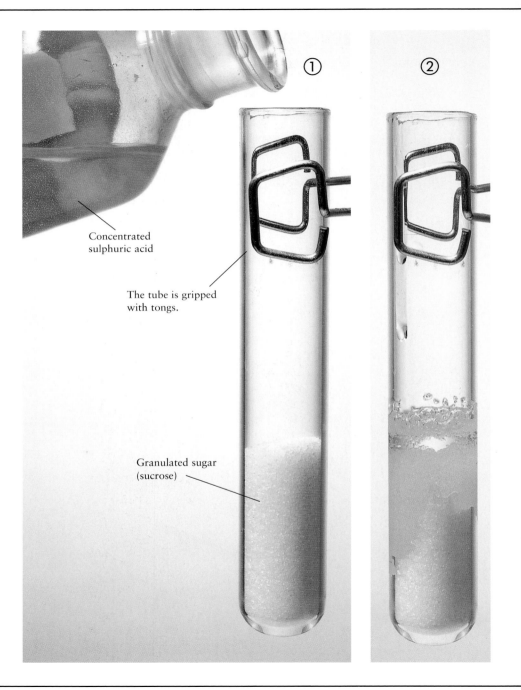

① ②

Concentrated sulphuric acid

The tube is gripped with tongs.

Granulated sugar (sucrose)

③ ④ ⑤

⑥

EQUATION: Dehydration of sucrose using concentrated sulphuric acid
Sucrose + concentrated sulphuric acid ⇨ steam + carbon + sulphuric acid
$C_{12}H_{22}O_{11}(s) + H_2SO_4(conc) ⇨ 11H_2O(g) + 12C(s) + H_2SO_4(aq)$
Heat given out

BASES

As with acids, bases are widely found in nature and have many applications in the home and the laboratory. Bases include the oxides and hydroxides of metals, which react with acids to form a salt and water only. Ammonia is also a base. A classic acid–base reaction is shown on page 16. For more information on salts, see page 48.

The history of base discovery

Like acids, bases have been in use since ancient times. A base such as quicklime (CaO, calcium oxide) which is produced by baking limestone has many useful properties: it is an important soil conditioner and one of the key components of mortar and is sometimes used to help decompose bodies quickly.

Sodium hydroxide ($NaOH$, caustic soda) is a strong base used as a degreasing agent for making soap and unblocking drains. It was traditionally prepared by adding slaked lime ($CaOH_2$, quicklime in water) to sodium carbonate (Na_2CO_3, which came from salt beds). It is now generally obtained by electrolysis of brine (see page 43).

But, although these bases were widely used, no one was sure how they worked or what relationship they had to acids.

In 1887, the link between bases and acids was made by the Swedish chemist, Svante Arrhenius. In his ionic theory (see page 8), a base was a substance that, if it dissolved in water, became ionised and released negatively charged hydroxide (OH^-) ions.

Acids and bases neutralise one another. The ionic theory of Arrhenius suggested that, if an acid releases positively charged hydrogen ions (H^+), then a base must release negatively charged ions to neutralise it. These negatively charged ions are hydroxide ions (OH^-). In this way, the ions of an acid and a base combine to produce water (H^+ and OH^- yield H_2O).

So, for example, hydrochloric acid (HCl) in water yields hydrogen (H^+) and chloride (Cl^-) ions. The base sodium hydroxide, is actually made of sodium (Na^+) and hydroxide (OH^-) ions. Put this acid and base together and the H^+ and OH^- ions form water, while the Cl^- and Na^+ ions make the neutral substance, or salt, sodium chloride, $NaCl$, which will crystallise out if the water is evaporated. (For more information on salts, see page 48.)

Most bases are insoluble. However, when a base dissolves in water, it forms an alkaline solution and is an ALKALI (see page 44). Alkalis turn litmus indicator blue, and can be as corrosive as acids. Alkalis were soon recognised by their bitter taste and their slippery and soapy feel. Some, such as sodium hydroxide, potassium hydroxide, calcium hydroxide (limewater) and ammonium hydroxide, are standard reagents found on the laboratory bench. (Note however, that in industry the word 'alkali' has a different meaning, being restricted to sodium hydroxide, sodium carbonate, and potassium carbonate.)

Properties of bases

Bases have a number of common properties:

(i) Bases react with and neutralise acids, producing a salt and water only (page 46).

(ii) Soluble bases precipitate metal hydroxides from metal salt solutions (page 46).

(iii) Soluble bases react with some metals to form a salt and release hydrogen (page 44).

(iv) Bases react with ammonium salts to release gaseous ammonia, a salt and water (page 48).

(v) Soluble bases make certain substances, called indicators, change colour. For example, purple litmus is turned blue by alkalis (page 64).

(Below) The diaphragm cell uses electrolysis in the manufacture of sodium hydroxide from brine. The brine is pumped in on the left side, where the cell is kept under pressure. Sodium hydroxide is drawn off on the right.

EQUATION: Electrolysis of a salt solution

Sodium chloride + water ⇨ sodium hydroxide + chlorine + hydrogen

$$2NaCl(aq) + 2H_2O(l) \rightsquigarrow 2NaOH(aq) + Cl_2(g) + H_2(g)$$

Electrical energy

Chloride ions are discharged to form molecules of chlorine (Cl_2), which is drawn off.

The diaphragm. Asbestos was the first material used, but modern cells use a form of plastic (polymer).

Hydrogen ions are discharged to form molecules of hydrogen gas (H_2), which is drawn off.

Strong brine is fed into the cell (usually pumped from rocks).

The positive electrode (anode) is made from titanium coated with platinum.

Sodium ions, together with hydroxide ions, from the water form sodium hydroxide.

Sodium ions from the brine pass through and concentrate the sodium hydroxide, leaving chloride ions.

Electricity supply

The negative electrode (cathode) is a perforated steel box.

More concentrated sodium hydroxide is produced.

MANUFACTURING A BASE

A wide range of bases are produced for use in industry. One of the most widely used is sodium hydroxide, caustic soda, and this is described here. It uses salt as its starting material.

One of the most important, efficient and elegant processes for getting products from salt involves passing an electric current through brine (a concentrated sodium chloride solution) in a container called a diaphragm cell.

The electrolytic cell is divided in half by a SEMIPERMEABLE MEMBRANE. Brine, containing sodium and chloride ions, is pumped into the cell. The semipermeable membrane is designed so that sodium ions can pass through, but the larger chloride ions cannot.

An electrical current attracts the sodium ions through the semipermeable membrane to the cathode, where, with hydroxide ions in the water, a solution of sodium hydroxide is formed.

NOTE: This process yields a number of other valuable products, such as hydrogen and chlorine in addition to the alkali.

Making an alkaline solution

Adding a soluble base such as sodium hydroxide to water produces an aqueous solution of the base. This solution is called an ALKALINE SOLUTION. Heat is produced (the process is exothermic) as the sodium hydroxide goes into solution.

Demonstration: dissolving sodium hydroxide in water

In this demonstration, some crystals of sodium hydroxide (caustic soda) are dropped into a beaker of cold, distilled water and stirred with a stirring thermometer (①). As the crystals of hydroxide dissolve in the water, the thermometer records a rapid rise in temperature, in this case by 10°C (②).

The presence of an alkaline solution can be tested, if desired, by dropping some Universal Indicator solution into the solution. It will turn blue.

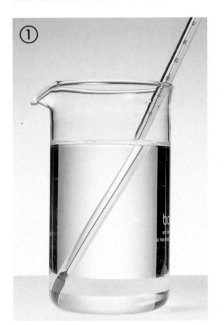

Reaction of alkalis with metals

Many metals do not react with alkalis. However, certain metals, including aluminium, zinc and lead, have amphoteric properties – that is, they react with both acids and alkalis.

Demonstration: reaction of sodium hydroxide with aluminium

Aluminium is an AMPHOTERIC metal. In this demonstration, a new aluminium pie dish is used (①).

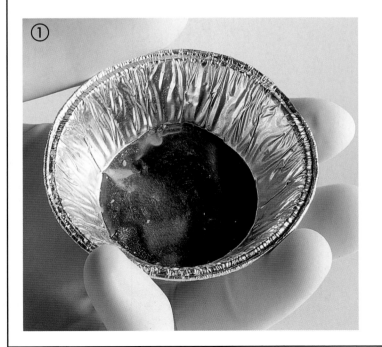

A small amount of concentrated sodium hydroxide is added and there is an immediate reaction (②).

The reaction releases hydrogen gas (the bubbles) and produces soluble sodium aluminate. The two form a froth (③).

The reaction destroys the bottom of the pie dish within a few minutes (④).

Remarks

The oxides and hydroxides of these metals are also amphoteric and the addition of sodium hydroxide to such compounds will also cause a reaction.

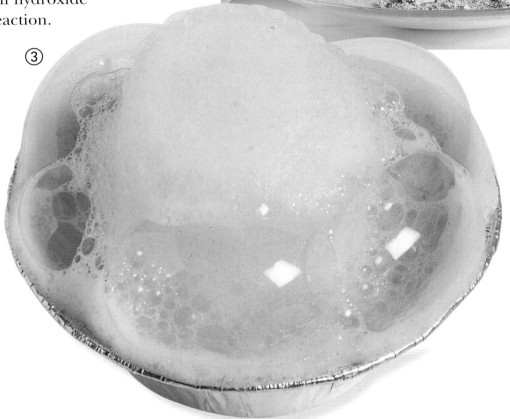

④

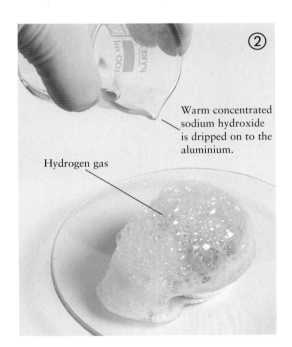

②

Warm concentrated sodium hydroxide is dripped on to the aluminium.

Hydrogen gas

③

EQUATION: Aluminium and sodium hydroxide

Aluminium + concentrated sodium hydroxide + water ⇨ sodium aluminate + hydrogen

$2Al(s) + 2NaOH(conc) + 6H_2O(l) ⇨ 2NaAl(OH)_4(aq) + 3H_2(g)$

Precipitation of metal hydroxides

It is a characteristic of alkalis (soluble bases) that they will precipitate insoluble metal hydroxides (bases) from metal salt solutions. Since these metal hydroxides are insoluble, they are not identified using an indicator. In fact, sodium hydroxide (page 40), potassium hydroxide, ammonia solution and calcium hydroxide are the only common soluble hydroxides.

Also, it is a general definition of a base that it will react with an acid to produce a salt and water only. This provides a useful identification for an insoluble base. All of the characteristics are shown with this example, using sodium hydroxide, iron(III) chloride and sulphuric acid.

③

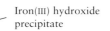
Iron(III) hydroxide precipitate

Demonstration: producing and identifying an insoluble base

Metal chlorides are salts and most metal chlorides are soluble (see also the section on salts, page 50). Iron(III) chloride forms a yellow aqueous solution.

In this demonstration, some iron(III) chloride is first poured into a Petri dish (①). A small amount of sodium hydroxide (alkali) is slowly dripped from a pipette into the iron(III) chloride solution (②).

Where the hydroxide and chloride react, a brown–red precipitate of iron(III) hydroxide immediately forms. This base is therefore characteristically insoluble. In this instance, only a small amount of

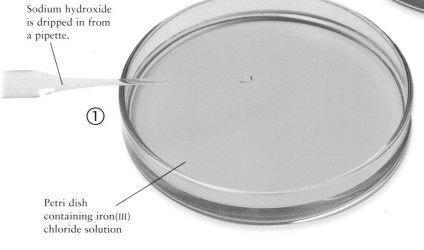

Sodium hydroxide is dripped in from a pipette.

①

Petri dish containing iron(III) chloride solution

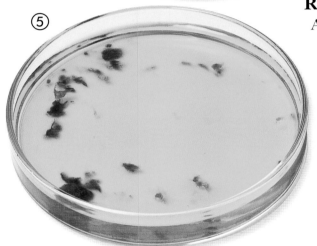

Dilute sulphuric acid

④

⑤

sodium hydroxide is added, and so a considerable amount of yellow iron(III) chloride solution remains in the Petri dish (③). If the sodium hydroxide is added to excess, the hydroxide precipitate does not redissolve.

The second part of the demonstration shows how a base reacts with an acid to form a salt.

Drops of dilute sulphuric acid are now added from a pipette (④). The iron(III) hydroxide reacts with the acid to form a soluble salt, yellow iron(III) sulphate solution (⑤). As a result, the brown–red precipitate disappears, leaving a mixture of iron(III) chloride and iron(III) sulphate as a pale yellow liquid (⑥).

Remarks

Adding an alkali, normally sodium hydroxide or ammonia solution, to metal salts, is a standard test for the metal ions present. The hydroxides that are precipitated have identifiable colours and textures. For example, iron(II) hydroxide is green and gelatinous, copper(II) hydroxide is blue and gelatinous, and lead hydroxide is white and granular.

⑥

The final solution is a mixture of colourless iron(III) sulphate and yellow iron(III) chloride.

EQUATION 1: Precipitating an insoluble base, iron(III) hydroxide
Sodium hydroxide + iron(III) chloride ⇨ iron(III) hydroxide + sodium chloride
$3NaOH(conc) + FeCl_3(aq) ⇨ Fe(OH)_3(s) + 3NaCl(aq)$
ALKALI + SOLUBLE METAL SALT ⇨ METAL HYDROXIDE PRECIPITATE

EQUATION 2: Reaction of an insoluble base with an acid
Sulphuric acid + iron(III) hydroxide ⇨ iron(III) sulphate + sodium chloride
$3H_2SO_4(aq) + 2Fe(OH)_3(s) ⇨ Fe_2(SO_4)_3(aq) + 6H_2O(l)$
ACID + BASE ⇨ SALT + WATER

The reaction of bases with ammonium salts

Strong bases, such as calcium hydroxide, act on ammonium salts to release gaseous ammonia, a salt and water.

Demonstration: reaction of calcium hydroxide with ammonium sulphate

Equal quantities of solid calcium hydroxide and ammonium sulphate are ground up and mixed using a pestle and mortar. The mixture is put into a long-necked, round-bottomed flask, and the neck clamped so that it points downwards (①).

The delivery tube is connected to an upturned funnel, using some rubber tubing. The funnel is submerged in distilled water in a beaker, and provides a large surface area for the ammonia gas to come in contact with the water. The mixture is heated and ammonia and water vapour are given off. The ammonia dissolves in the water in the beaker, producing the alkali, ammonium hydroxide.

The presence of ammonia can be tested for by dipping a filter paper in hydrochloric acid and placing it just above the water. As ammonia is released from the water, the reaction of the

ammonia and the escaping hydrogen chloride gas produces a characteristic white smoke of ammonium chloride.

Remarks

Ammonia is an extremely soluble alkaline gas that is often found in solution as the alkaline laboratory reagent called ammonia solution (ammonium hydroxide).

EQUATION: Reaction of calcium hydroxide with ammonium sulphate
Calcium hydroxide + ammonium sulphate ⇨ ammonia + calcium sulphate + water
$Ca(OH)_2(s) + (NH_4)_2SO_4(s) ⇨ 2NH_3(g) + CaSO_4(s) + 2H_2O(l)$
BASE + AMMONIUM SALT ⇨ AMMONIA + SALT + WATER

SALTS

Salts are the products (along with water) of a reaction between an acid and a base. Salts are common in nature, making up most of the materials of the Earth's crust, as well as the materials dissolved in the oceans. They include such compounds as sodium chloride (NaCl), galena (PbS) and calcium carbonate ($CaCO_3$). However, many more are made by the chemical industry. (NOTE: Do not confuse the term salt, as used in a chemical sense, with the common term salt, which is restricted to the salt we use in food, sodium chloride. For example, the sea contains a wide variety of dissolved salts, only one of which is sodium chloride.)

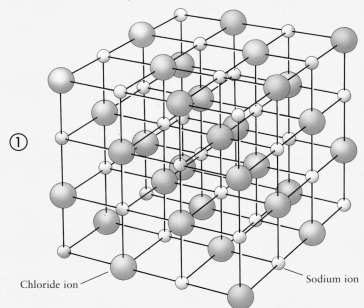

①

Chloride ion — Sodium ion

(Above) **Sodium chloride is a salt. As a solid, the sodium and chloride ions of the compound form a cubic crystalline structure** *(right).*

Characteristics of salts

In general, salts are found as solids. They are made of ions, bonded together in crystalline structures (①).

Most salts are characterised by having high melting and boiling points. The colour of a salt in solution tends to mirror the characteristic colour of the metal ion (thus, for example, most copper(II) salt solutions are blue. However, the nature of the acid radical can make a difference).

Formation of salts

A salt is produced when hydrogen ions in an acid are replaced by metal ions such as sodium (Na^+) ions or ammonium (NH_4^+) ions. Thus salts may be produced as a result of a reaction between acids and bases. Salts were originally defined as one of the products of the reaction of acids with bases, the other product being water. This kind of reaction is known as neutralisation. For example:

Hydrochloric acid + sodium hydroxide ⇨ *sodium chloride + water*
$HCl(aq) + NaOH(aq)$ ⇨ $NaCl(aq) + H_2O(l)$
ACID + BASE ⇨ SALT + WATER

But, a reaction of an acid and a base is not the only way to produce a salt. For example, a reaction between hydrochloric acid (HCl) and metallic zinc (Zn) yields the salt zinc chloride (ZnCl) and hydrogen gas (see page 11):

Hydrochloric acid + zinc ⇨ *zinc chloride + hydrogen gas*
$2HCl(aq) + Zn(s)$ ⇨ $ZnCl_2(aq) + H_2(g)$
ACID + METAL ⇨ SALT + HYDROGEN

It is also possible to form salts by combining elements directly, a process known as 'SYNTHESIS'. Thus iron (Fe) and sulphur (S) combine to form the salt, iron(II) sulphide (FeS) (②).

Iron + sulphur ⇨ *iron(II) sulphide*
$Fe(s) + S(s)$ ⇨ $FeS(s)$

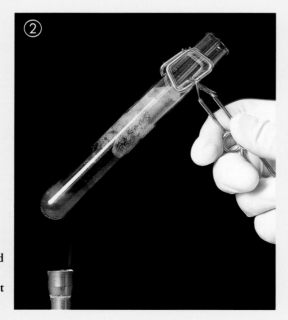

②

(Right) If sulphur and iron filings are mixed in a boiling tube and heated in a Bunsen flame they will react to form the salt iron(II) sulphide.

Salts can also be formed by replacing the negatively charged hydroxide (OH⁻) of a base with non-metallic ions such as chloride (Cl⁻), or with other negatively charged ions such as sulphate (SO₄⁻).

One salt can be converted into another when salts combine in solution. For example, if the salt, barium chloride, is added to a solution containing the salt, sodium sulphate, the salts exchange ions, the barium sulphate precipitates and the remaining solution contains sodium chloride.

The exchange occurs because the energy of the salts after exchange is lower than the energy of the salts before interchange. The exchange can result in the formation of a precipitate, or the mixing of the salts, as two solids can result in the formation of liquid products:

Barium chloride + sodium sulphate ⇨ *barium sulphate + sodium chloride*
$BaCl_2(aq) + Na_2SO_4(aq)$ ⇨ $BaSO_4(s) + NaCl(aq)$

Properties of a salt

Because salts always consist of ions bonded together, they can, like acids and bases, dissociate in a solvent, and act as electrolytes when molten.

Kinds and names of salts

Salts can be of three kinds: normal, acid, or basic. Salts can also be inorganic or organic, depending on the acid used in their formation.

Normal salts: An example of a NORMAL SALT is sodium chloride (NaCl). These neutral salts do not contain a hydroxide (OH⁻) ion, which would make them basic salts, or a hydrogen ion, which would make them acid salts.

A normal salt has a name made up of the metal from which it is formed, and a suffix, indicating the kind of salt it is. An -ide suffix is used if the negative ion does not contain any oxygen (e.g. sodium chloride, $NaCl$). A salt that contains oxygen may end in the suffixes -ate or -ite. Those salts ending in -ate have more oxygen than those ending in -ite. For example, sodium sulphate (Na_2SO_4) is produced using sulphuric acid (H_2SO_4), whereas sodium sulphite is produced using sulphurous acid (H_2SO_3).

Acid salts: An ACID SALT contains at least one hydrogen ion. The hydrogen ion can then behave as an acid in chemical reactions.

Acid salts are produced under conditions that do not allow complete neutralisation of the acid. For example, sulphuric acid may react with a sodium compound to produce a normal sodium salt, sodium sulphate (Na_2SO_4), or it may retain some of the hydrogen, in which case it becomes the salt, sodium hydrogen sulphate ($NaHSO_4$).

Basic salts: A BASIC SALT contains at least one hydroxide ion. The hydroxide ion can then behave as a base in chemical reactions.

For example, the reaction of hydrochloric acid (HCl) with the base, aluminium hydroxide ($Al(OH)_3$), usually produces the normal salt aluminium chloride ($AlCl_3$), but two basic salts, $Al(OH)_2Cl$ and $Al(OH)Cl_2$, may also form.

Recognising a salt
Any metal chloride, carbonate, nitrate or sulphate will be a salt.

Solubility of salts
Many salts are soluble. However, a few, including important and widely occurring salts such as calcium carbonate, are insoluble (③).
- All salts of potassium, sodium and ammonium are soluble in water.
- All nitrates are soluble in water.
- Most chlorides are soluble in water (lead and silver chlorides are the common exceptions).
- Most sulphates are soluble in water (barium and lead sulphates are the common exceptions).
- Most carbonates are insoluble in water (sodium, potassium and ammonium are the common exceptions).

③	THE SOLUBILITY OF SALTS			
Element	Chloride	Nitrate	Sulphate	Carbonate
Ammonium ion	S	S	S	S
Potassium	S	S	S	S
Sodium	S	S	S	S
Barium	S	S	I	I
Calcium	S	S	SL	I
Magnesium	S	S	S	I
Zinc	S	S	S	I
Iron(II)	S	S	S	I
Lead(II)	I	S	I	I
Copper(II)	S	S	S	I
Silver	I	S	SL	I

I = insoluble   SL = slightly soluble   S = soluble

Preparing an insoluble salt

An insoluble salt can be made by precipitation. Two suitable aqueous solutions are mixed together so that the insoluble salt precipitates, as shown here.

Demonstration: preparation of an insoluble salt by mixing two soluble salts

In this demonstration, the insoluble salt, Prussian blue (potassium iron(III) hexacyanoferrate(II)) is produced by reacting two soluble salts.

One of the salts to be chosen as a reactant must contain ions of the metal in the desired insoluble salt. In this case, iron(III) ions are required and iron(III) chloride is used.

The other salt used must contain the non-metal ion of the desired insoluble salt and, in this case, potassium hexacyanoferrate(II) is used.

The pale yellow solution of potassium hexacyanoferrate(II) is poured into a beaker and placed on a magnetic stirrer. This spins a plastic-coated metal mixer (sometimes called a magnetic flea) in the bottom of the beaker, setting up a vortex in the solution (①).

Some yellow iron(III) chloride is then added from a pipette and, where the two reactants mix in the centre of the vortex, a blue suspension appears (②). This is an insoluble precipitate of Prussian blue. The stirring process eventually produces an even reaction throughout the beaker (③ & ④).

The iron(III) ions (Fe^{3+}) and the hexacyanoferrate(II) ions ($Fe(CN)_6^{4-}$) have combined to form the insoluble salt, Prussian blue or potassium iron(III) hexacyanoferrate(II). The potassium (K^+) and chloride (Cl^-) ions play no part in the reaction, and so are called SPECTATOR IONS.

Pipette containing iron(III) chloride

Beaker containing potassium hexacyanoferrate(II)

①

Magnetic stirrer

Spinning magnetic flea

EQUATION: Precipitation of an insoluble salt, Prussian blue

Iron(III) chloride + potassium hexacyanoferrate(II) ⇨ *potassium iron(III) hexacyanoferrate(II) + potassium chloride*

$FeCl_3(aq) + K_4[Fe(CN)_6](aq)$ ⇨ $KFe[Fe(CN)_6](s) + 3KCl(aq)$

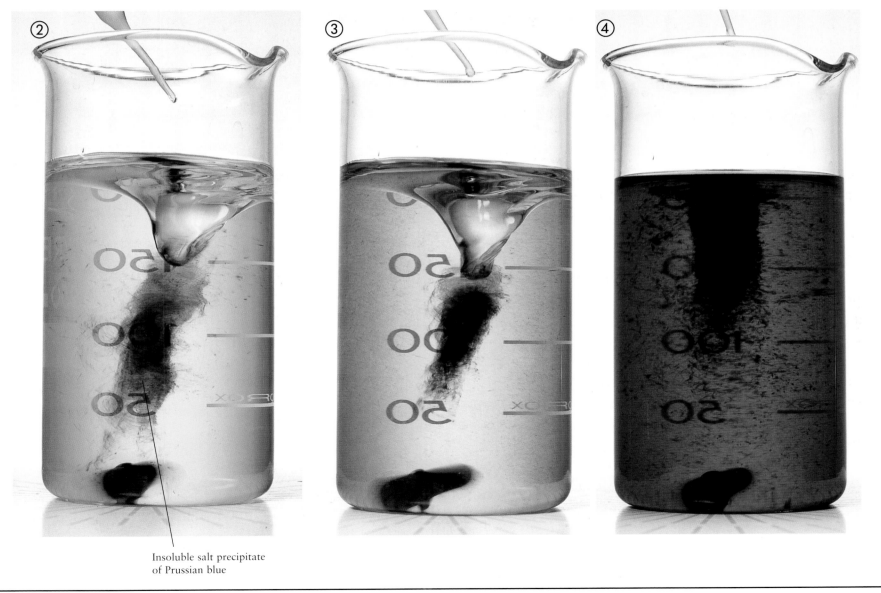

Insoluble salt precipitate
of Prussian blue

Preparing a soluble salt

Soluble salts can be prepared from metals, metal oxides or hydroxides (bases), soluble metal hydroxides (an alkali) or metal carbonates. The acid used determines the salt that will be formed. Thus, if the salt is to be a chloride, then hydrochloric acid (HCl) must be used; if the salt is to be a sulphate, then sulphuric acid (H_2SO_4) must be used; and if the salt is to be a nitrate, then nitric acid (HNO_3) must be used.

Each reaction produces a distinctive range of products:
• Metal oxide or hydroxide (a base) and an acid yield a salt and water (shown on this page).
• Metal and acid yield a salt and hydrogen gas (see pages 11 to 14).
• Metal carbonate and an acid yield a salt and water and give off carbon dioxide gas (see pages 18 to 20).

Demonstration: preparation of a soluble salt by reaction of an acid with an oxide

The salt, copper(II) sulphate, can be prepared by reacting black copper(II) oxide with dilute sulphuric acid (①). The resulting translucent, blue, copper(II) sulphate solution can be evaporated to obtain hydrated copper(II) sulphate crystals (②). Small crystals will be produced unless a seed crystal is introduced at this point (③).

EQUATION: Preparing a soluble salt from an acid and a base
Dilute sulphuric acid + copper(II) oxide ⇨ copper(II) sulphate + water
$H_2SO_4(aq) + CuO(s) ⇨ CuSO_4(aq) + H_2O(l)$
ACID   +   BASE   ⇨   SALT   +   WATER

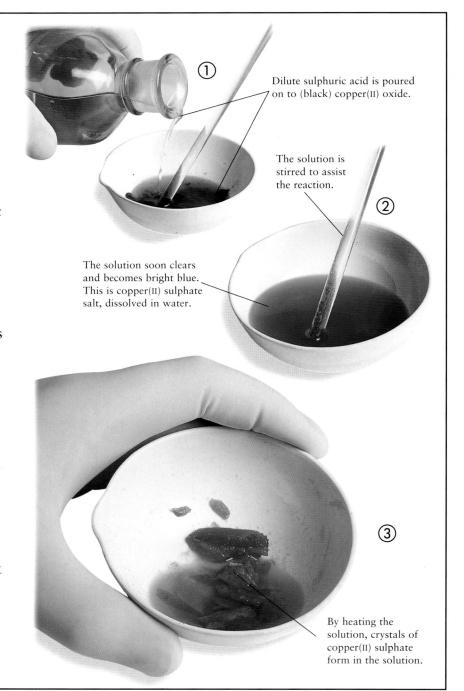

① Dilute sulphuric acid is poured on to (black) copper(II) oxide.

The solution is stirred to assist the reaction. ②

The solution soon clears and becomes bright blue. This is copper(II) sulphate salt, dissolved in water.

③

By heating the solution, crystals of copper(II) sulphate form in the solution.

Titration to produce salts

A soluble salt can be obtained by TITRATION. A titration is a quantitative method used to add exactly the right amount of acid to an alkali (or vice versa) to cause neutralisation and thereby produce a salt. Care has to be taken to make sure that the measurements are accurate.

Demonstration: titration of hydrochloric acid with sodium hydroxide

The apparatus used is shown in the diagram (①). The first stage is to fill the burette, including the space (known as the dead space) below the tap, by gradually releasing liquid out of the base of the burette until the dead space has been filled (② & ③, page 56). If desired, more liquid can then be run out of the burette to bring the level of the meniscus in the burette to the zero mark (④, page 56), or the starting level of the liquid can simply be read from the graduated tube.

The important part of a titration is the end point, when a measured amount of acid has neutralised by a measured amount of alkali. At this point, the salt is produced. It is therefore critical to the success of the method that this end point is arrived at with great accuracy.

To show this most clearly, this demonstration uses a small amount of acid solution in a Petri dish, and an alkali in the burette; but if larger quantities are to be titrated, then the acid would be in a flask. Similarly, the

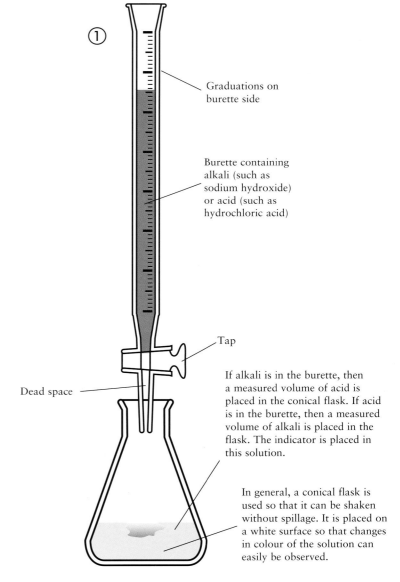

①

Graduations on burette side

Burette containing alkali (such as sodium hydroxide) or acid (such as hydrochloric acid)

Tap

Dead space

If alkali is in the burette, then a measured volume of acid is placed in the conical flask. If acid is in the burette, then a measured volume of alkali is placed in the flask. The indicator is placed in this solution.

In general, a conical flask is used so that it can be shaken without spillage. It is placed on a white surface so that changes in colour of the solution can easily be observed.

EQUATION: Titration of hydrochloric acid and sodium hydroxide
Hydrochloric acid + sodium hydroxide ⇨ sodium chloride + water
$HCl(aq) + NaOH(aq) ⇨ NaCl(aq) + H_2O(l)$

acid could be in the burette and the alkali in the flask (chosen so that it can be shaken without spillage).

The end point can be determined using a colour indicator, as shown here (⑤), or by using a pH meter, in which case the titration is continued until the meter shows a sudden change in pH through neutral.

In this demonstration, phenolphthalein was used as the indicator and was added to the acid solution in the Petri dish (chosen to be clear for these photographs). Phenolphthalein turns pink when alkaline (8 to 10 on the pH scale). Initially, the phenolphthalein in the acidic solution remains colourless (⑥).

To see how the titration works, a few drops of alkali from the burette are dripped into the solution in the dish. For a short time, the effect of the alkali is to trigger a colour response in the indicator. A flash of pink is seen where the drops enter the acid, but quickly disappears (⑦).

Over a few minutes, with the burette being allowed to drip slowly, most of the acid is neutralised and the pink flash of colour lasts longer and becomes more extensive (⑧). However, this pink patch can be dispersed easily with stirring (⑨, see page 58).

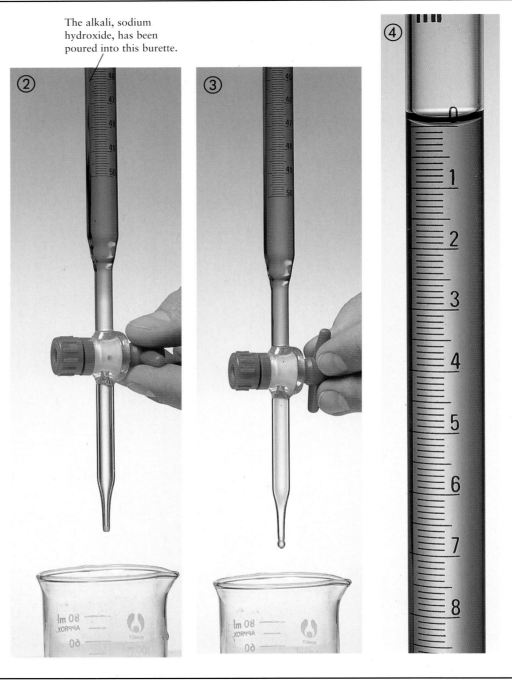

The alkali, sodium hydroxide, has been poured into this burette.

② ③ ④

56

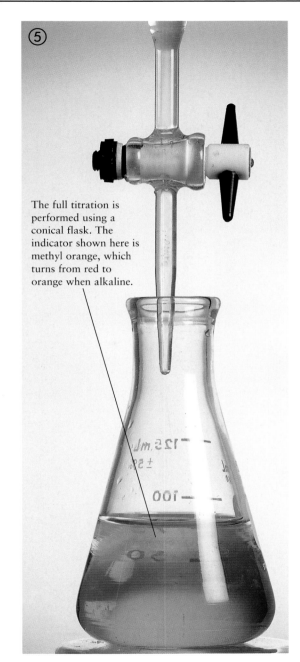

⑤ The full titration is performed using a conical flask. The indicator shown here is methyl orange, which turns from red to orange when alkaline.

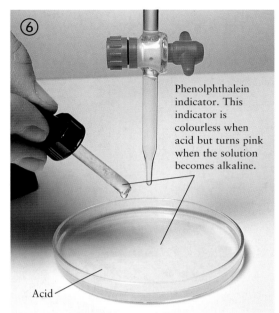

⑥ Phenolphthalein indicator. This indicator is colourless when acid but turns pink when the solution becomes alkaline.

Acid

⑦ Where the solution is alkaline, the indicator turns pink. However, before the end point is reached, the pink spot can be dispersed by stirring (see ⑧ and ⑨).

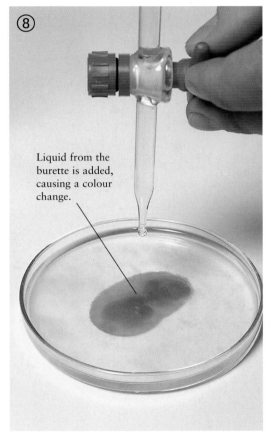

⑧ Liquid from the burette is added, causing a colour change.

As the end point is reached, the pink colour remains as a patch that does not disperse easily. When this stage is reached, the drop rate needs to be reduced. As more alkali is added, the pink-coloured patch becomes more difficult to disperse (⑩). The end point is finally reached when the pink colour can no longer be dispersed by stirring (⑪). It may only require one drop to cause this transition from colourless to permanently pink. The acid has now been neutralised and a soluble salt has been produced.

Stirring the solution with a glass rod disperses the colour.

DEMONSTRATION

To find the volume of an acid solution (of known concentration) that reacts with a known volume of an alkaline solution (of known concentration) to produce a salt, the procedure is as follows:

25 cm³ of 2M (M = moles per litre, or mol/l) hydrochloric acid is placed in the flask.

The burette is filled with 2M sodium hydroxide solution.

In this demonstration the end point was reached when 25.1 cm³ of sodium hydroxide had been added to the 25 cm³ of acid (i.e. a 1:1 reaction).

The equation for the reaction is:
Hydrochloric acid + sodium hydroxide ⇨ *sodium chloride + water*
$HCl(aq) + NaOH(aq)$ ⇨ $NaCl(aq) + H_2O(l)$

The equation shows that the same number of moles of hydrogen chloride as of sodium hydroxide are required to produce a neutral solution. It should therefore take 25 cm³ of 2M sodium hydroxide to produce a neutral salt solution. This is the volume of sodium hydroxide we would therefore expect to have to add from the burette.

⑩

As the end point is reached, it becomes more difficult to disperse the colour but, until the end point is reached, the solution turns back to being colourless when stirred.

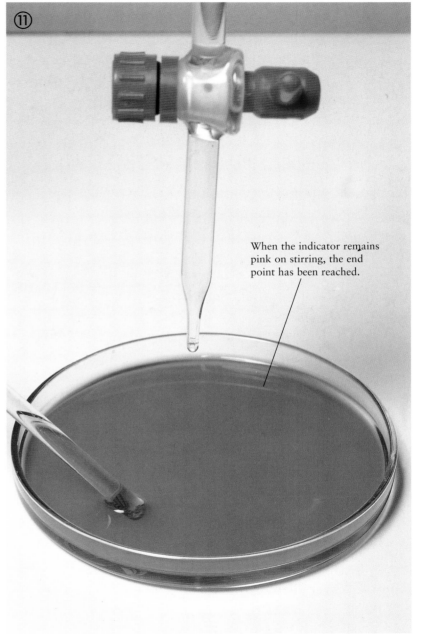

⑪

When the indicator remains pink on stirring, the end point has been reached.

The electrical conductivity of acids, bases and salts

The stronger the acid or base, the more conducting are the ions that are present and the better it conducts electricity. If an acid and base are reacted then, at the point at which they neutralise one another (the neutralisation point or end point) and form a salt, the solution will have its lowest conductivity.

Demonstration: measuring conductivity changes during the preparation of a salt

The apparatus used in this demonstration is designed to measure the electrical conductivity of the solution during the reaction between sodium hydroxide (a soluble base or alkali) and sulphuric acid (①).

A conductivity cell is set up using the same apparatus as would be used for electrolysis. This consists of a glass container, the cell, in which two electrodes are placed. The electrodes are connected to a Direct Current (DC) electrical source and an ammeter to record electrical current passing through the solution. The pH of the solution can also be recorded using a pH meter (not shown).

A burette is filled with dilute sulphuric acid and placed over the conductivity cell. A measured volume of sodium hydroxide solution is then added to the cell using a graduated pipette (②), and the first ammeter reading of the electrical current is recorded (③). The pH is also recorded.

A small volume of acid, in this case 2.5 cm³, is run into the cell (④). The solution is stirred, and the ammeter (⑤) and pH meter are then read again. This procedure is repeated for additional acid volumes of 2.5 cm³ (⑥, ⑦ & ⑧). The graph on page 61 shows the changes observed.

As more acid is added, and the solution becomes less alkaline, the ammeter readings and therefore the conductivity of the solution declines. When the

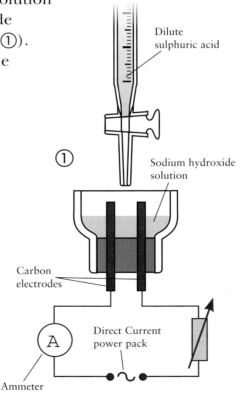

① Dilute sulphuric acid

Sodium hydroxide solution

Carbon electrodes

Ammeter

Direct Current power pack

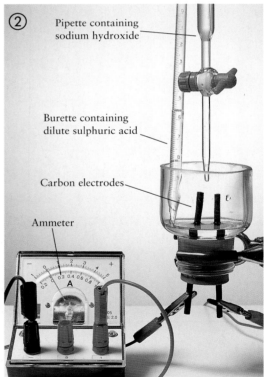

② Pipette containing sodium hydroxide

Burette containing dilute sulphuric acid

Carbon electrodes

Ammeter

solution is neutral, at pH 7, the conductivity is at its lowest. At this neutralisation point, all of the hydrogen ions in the acid added will have been neutralised by all of the hydroxide ions in the sodium hydroxide. The only residual conductivity could be produced by the sodium and sulphate ions, which have a lower conductivity.

As more acid is added after complete neutralisation has occurred, the solution becomes progressively more acidic, as shown by the declining pH. The conductivity increases again, showing that the higher the acidity, the more (hydrogen) ions there are present to conduct electricity.

Remarks

This demonstration can be repeated both for insoluble salts and soluble salts, and the results compared.

For an insoluble salt such as barium sulphate, the conductivity would fall to almost zero at the end point.

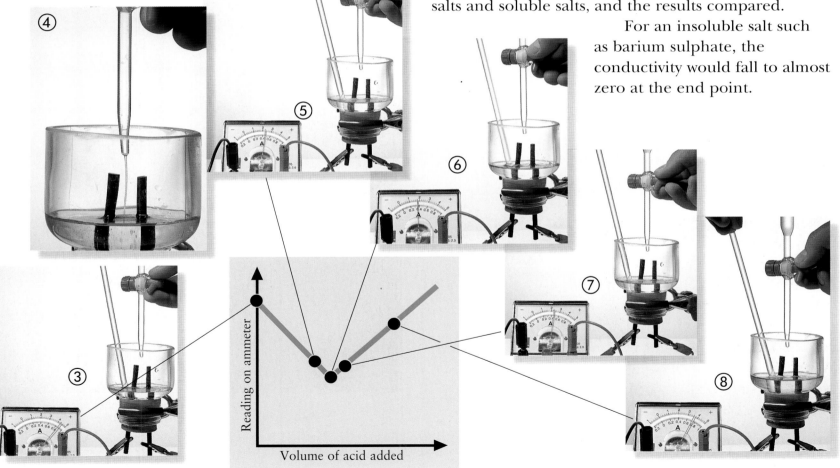

Preparation of a salt by the direct reaction of elements

The halogens (fluorine, chlorine, bromine and iodine) are very reactive elements and they will react with many metals to form salts. Once triggered by heating, these are extremely exothermic reactions. The reaction of sodium with the halogen, chlorine, needs little heating and is very violent producing sodium chloride. In these demonstrations, chlorine is reacted with the less reactive metals, iron and aluminium.

Demonstration 1: reaction of aluminium and chlorine

The apparatus consists of a system for generating chlorine, a combustion tube in which the aluminium is heated, and a collecting vessel, in this case a side-arm conical flask connected to a suction pump that will allow the chlorine to flow through the apparatus and also remove any unreacted chlorine at the end of the reaction (①). As chlorine gas is poisonous, all of the apparatus is placed in a fume chamber during the demonstration.

Chlorine gas is first generated by reacting concentrated hydrochloric acid from a dropper funnel with potassium permanganate in the conical flask and is then fed into a combustion tube (made of a heat-resistant glass) containing aluminium foil.

The aluminium foil is heated strongly and eventually it begins to flare (③). An intense white light

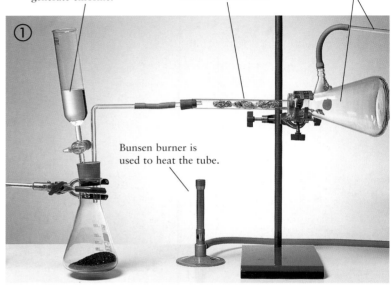

The dropper funnel allows for a controlled release of hydrochloric acid on to the potassium permanganate to generate chlorine.

The aluminium foil has been pushed into a glass tube. The chlorine is passed over the aluminium foil.

A suction pump draws off waste fumes from a side-arm flask.

Bunsen burner is used to heat the tube.

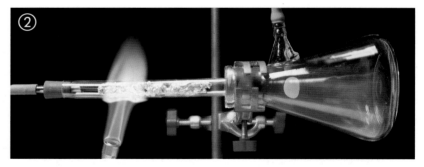

EQUATION: Reaction of aluminium and chlorine
Aluminium + chlorine ⇨ aluminium(III) chloride
$2Al(s) + 3Cl_2(g) ⇨ 2AlCl_3(s)$
SALT

appears from the burning aluminium, while a pale yellow smoke, consisting of fine particles of aluminium chloride, flows into the flask. A pale yellow crust of the salt aluminium chloride is left as a deposit inside the tube (③) and in the side-arm flask.

Demonstration 2: reaction of iron with chlorine

Chlorine will react with iron (in the form of steel wool) that is strongly heated to produce a large amount of reddish smoke, which is the salt, iron chloride.

The apparatus is identical to that used for aluminium, except that steel wool is used in place of aluminium foil.

The steel wool is heated strongly (④) and eventually it begins to flare up into yellow and red colours, the flaring section slowly making its way along the tube as the iron is consumed (⑤).

Reddish smoke containing the salt in the form of tiny iron(III) chloride particles begins to form and flows out to the collecting flask, gradually precipitating on the bottom of the flask.

③

Aluminium(III) chloride

④

EQUATION: Reaction of iron and chlorine
Iron + chlorine ⇨ iron(III) chloride
$2Fe(s) + 3Cl_2(g) \Rightarrow 2FeCl_3(s)$
SALT

⑤

Acid–base indicators

On the previous pages, an acid has been shown to be substance that releases hydrogen ions when it is in an AQUEOUS SOLUTION. Acids can therefore be identified by the presence of hydrogen ions in the solution. The concentration or strength of the acid can also be determined by the concentration of hydrogen ions, and this is measured on the pH scale.

The pH scale measures the hydrogen ion concentration in an aqueous solution. At 25°C, an acidic solution has a pH value less than 7; a basic solution (alkali) has a pH greater than 7; and a neutral, aqueous, solution has a pH equal to 7.

Using a pH meter

The pH meter consists of a meter and a probe. The probe is placed in the solution to be tested. As cross-contamination will occur if the probe is taken directly from one solution into another, it is vital that the probe is washed thoroughly in distilled water between tests.

The pH meter has to be calibrated before use. This involves using two BUFFER solutions. These are solutions that are resistant to changing pH. The buffers are made up using tablets, which are dropped

The meaning of pH

The acidity of a solution depends on the relative number of hydrogen (H^+) ions and hydroxide (OH^-) ions in the solution. This number varies enormously between very acid and very alkaline solutions, so it is not possible to use a simple straight line (linear) scale to measure the concentration. Instead, the pH scale is a logarithmic scale, where each number on the scale represents a tenfold change in concentration. Thus a pH 5 solution has ten times the hydrogen ion concentration of a pH 6 solution, and a pH 4 solution has 100 times the concentration of hydrogen ions of a pH 6 solution. On this scale, a pH of 1 is very strongly acidic, a pH of 14 is very strongly alkaline, and a pH of 7 is neutral.

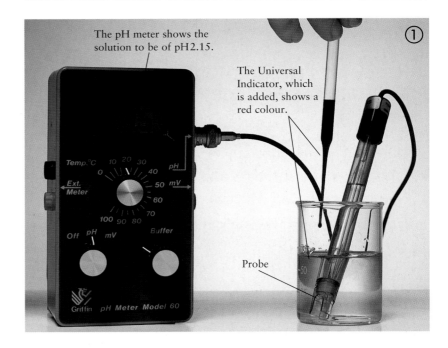

The pH meter shows the solution to be of pH2.15.

The Universal Indicator, which is added, shows a red colour.

Probe

Griffin pH Meter Model 60

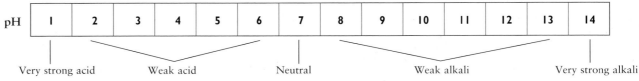

(Right) This chart shows the range of pH from a very strong acid at pH 1 to a very strong alkali at pH 14.

pH	1	2	3	4	5	6	7	8	9	10	11	12	13	14

Very strong acid   Weak acid   Neutral   Weak alkali   Very strong alkali into water and allowed to dissolve. Buffer solutions are made up to have known pH values from near the ends of the pH range. Once the calibration has been completed, the probe can be placed in any aqueous solution, and the pH determined immediately from the meter scale.

Here, an unknown colourless solution is tested and found to have a pH of 2.15 (①), showing it to be strongly acidic. This is then confirmed in an approximate way by dropping some (green) Universal Indicator into the solution and watching it turn red.

Indicators

The concentration of hydrogen ions can be measured with a chemical indicator. At a specific pH, an indicator will change colour. The traditional testing agent for the presence of an acid or a base used to be litmus solution. Its neutral colour is somewhere between blue and red. An acid solution causes it to change to red. An alkaline solution causes it to change to blue. However, litmus cannot indicate the pH, but only whether a solution is acid or alkaline (②).

Universal Indicator

There are many indicators in addition to litmus, most of which change colour at a specific pH. It is therefore possible to find out the pH of a solution by seeing which indicator changes colour. To make this process

as easy as possible, a number of indicator solutions are mixed together to make Universal Indicator. In the bottle, the Universal Indicator is deep green, but when a few drops are added to a solution of acid or alkali, it changes colour. Deep red indicates a very acidic solution, whereas bright blue indicates a very alkaline solution.

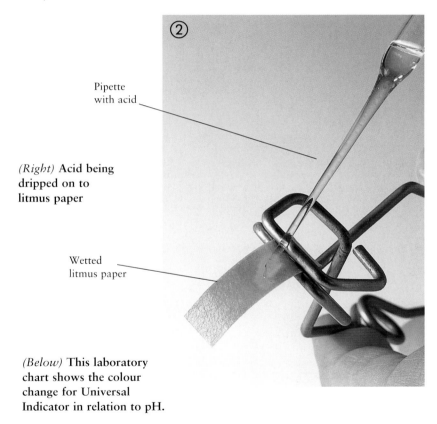

Pipette with acid

(Right) **Acid being dripped on to litmus paper**

Wetted litmus paper

(Below) **This laboratory chart shows the colour change for Universal Indicator in relation to pH.**

pH1 pH2 pH3 pH4 pH5 pH6 pH7 pH8 pH9 pH10 pH11

MASTER GLOSSARY

absolute zero: the lowest possible temperature ($-273.15°C$).

absorption: the process by which a substance is soaked up. *See:* adsorption.

acid: a substance that can give a proton to another substance. Acids are compounds, containing hydrogen, that can attack and dissolve many substances. Acids are described as weak or strong, dilute or concentrated, mineral or organic. *Example:* hydrochloric acid (HCl) An acid in water can react with a base to form a salt and water.

acidic solution: a solution with a pH lower than 7.

acidity: a general term for the strength of an acid in a solution.

acid radical: the negative ion left behind when an acid loses a hydrogen ion. *Example:* Cl^- in hydrochloric acid (HCl).

acid salt: An ACID SALT contains at least one hydrogen ion and can behave as an acid in chemical reactions. Acid salts are produced under conditions that do not allow complete neutralisation of the acid. For example, sulphuric acid may react with a sodium compound to produce a normal sodium salt, sodium sulphate (Na_2SO_4), or it may retain some of the hydrogen, in which case it becomes the salt sodium hydrogen sulphate ($NaHSO_4$).

actinide series or actinide metals: a series of 15 similar radioactive elements between actinium and lawrencium. They are transition metals.

activated charcoal: a form of carbon, made up of tiny crystals of graphite, which is made by heating organic matter in the absence of air. It is then processed further to increase its pore space and therefore its surface area. Its surface area is about 2000 m^2/g. Activated charcoal readily adsorbs many gases and it is therefore widely used as a filter, for example, in gas masks.

activation energy: the energy required to make a reaction occur. The greater the activation energy of a reaction, the more its reaction rate depends on temperature. The activation energy of a reaction is useful because, if the rate of reaction is known at one temperature (for example, 100 °C) then the activation energy can be used to calculate the rate of reaction at another temperature (for example, 400 °C) without actually doing the experiment.

adsorption: the process by which a surface adsorbs a substance. The substances involved are not chemically combined and can be separated. *Example:* the adsorption properties of activated charcoal. *See:* absorption.

alchemy: the traditional 'art' of working with chemicals that prevailed through the Middle Ages. One of the main challenges for alchemists was to make gold from lead. Alchemy faded away as scientific chemistry was developed in the 17th century.

alcohol: an organic compound which contains a hydroxyl (OH) group. *Example:* ethanol (CH_3CH_2OH), also known as ethyl alcohol or grain alcohol.

alkali/alkaline: a base in (aqueous) solution. Alkalis react with, or neutralise, hydrogen ions in acids and have a pH greater than 7.0 because they contain relatively few hydrogen ions. *Example:* aqueous sodium hydroxide (NaOH).

alkaline cell (or battery): a dry cell in which the electrolyte contains sodium or potassium hydroxide.

alkaline earth metal: a member of Group 2 of the Periodic Table. *Example:* calcium.

alkali metals: a member of Group 1 of the Periodic Table. *Example:* sodium.

alkane: a hydrocarbon with no carbon-to-carbon multiple bonds. *Example:* ethane, C_2H_6.

alkene: a hydrocarbon with at least one carbon-to-carbon double bond. *Example:* ethene, C_2H_4.

alkyne: a hydrocarbon with at least one carbon-to-carbon triple bond. *Example:* ethyne, C_2H_2.

allotropes: alternative forms of an element that differ in the way the atoms are linked. *Example:* white and red phosphorus.

alloy: a mixture of a metal and various other elements. *Example:* brass is an alloy of copper and zinc.

amalgam: a liquid alloy of mercury with another metal.

amorphous: a solid in which the atoms are not arranged regularly (i.e. glassy). Compare crystalline.

amphoteric: a metal that will react with both acids and alkalis. *Example:* aluminium metal.

anhydrous: lacking water; water has been removed, for example, by heating. Many hydrated salts are crystalline. (Opposite of anhydrous is hydrous or hydrated.) *Example:* copper(II) sulphate can be anhydrous ($CuSO_4$) or hydrated ($CuSO_4 \cdot 5H_2O$).

anion: a negatively charged atom or group of atoms. *Examples:* chloride ion (Cl^-), hydroxide ion (OH^-).

anode: the electrode at which oxidation occurs; the negative terminal of a battery or the positive electrode of an electrolysis cell.

anodising: a process that uses the effect of electrolysis to make a surface corrosion resistant. *Example:* anodised aluminium.

antacid: a common name for any compound that reacts with stomach acid to neutralise it. *Example:* sodium hydrogen carbonate, also known as sodium bicarbonate.

antioxidant: a substance that reacts rapidly with radicals thereby preventing oxidation of some other substance.

anti-bumping granules: small glass or ceramic beads, designed to promote boiling without the development of large gas bubbles.

approximate relative atomic mass: *See:* relative atomic mass.

aqueous: a solution in which the solvent is water. Usually used as 'aqueous solution'. *Example:* aqueous solution of sodium hydroxide (NaOH(aq)).

aromatic hydrocarbons: compounds of carbon that have the benzene ring as part of their structure. *Examples:* benzene (C_6H_6), naphthalene ($C_{10}H_8$). They are known as aromatic because of the strong pungent smell given off by benzene.

atmospheric pressure: the pressure exerted by the gases in the air. Units of measurement are kilopascals (kPa), atmospheres (atm), millimetres of mercury (mm Hg) and Torr. Standard atmospheric pressure is 100 kPa, 1atm, 760 mm Hg or 760 Torr.

atom: the smallest particle of an element; a nucleus and its surrounding electrons.

atomic mass: the mass of an atom measured in atomic mass units (amu). An atomic mass unit is equal to one-twelfth of the atom of carbon-12. Atomic mass is now more generally used instead of atomic weight. *Example:* the atomic mass of chlorine is about 35 amu. *See:* atomic weight, relative atomic mass.

atomic number: also known as proton number. The number of electrons or the number of protons in an atom. *Example:* the atomic number of gold is 79 and for carbon it is 4.

atomic structure: the nucleus and the arrangement of electrons around the nucleus of an atom.

atomic weight: a common term used to mean the average molar mass of an element. This is the mass per mole of atoms. *Example:* the atomic weight of chlorine is about 35 g/mol. *See:* atomic mass, mole.

base: a substance that can accept a proton from another substance. *Example:* aqueous ammonia ($NH_3(aq)$). A base can react with an acid in water to form a salt and water.

basic salt: a salt that contains at least one hydroxide ion. The hydroxide ion can then behave as a base in chemical reactions. *Example:* the reaction of hydrochloric acid (HCl) with the base, aluminium hydroxide ($Al(OH)_3$) can form two basic salts, $Al(OH)_2Cl$ and $Al(OH)Cl_2$.

battery: a number of electrochemical cells placed in series.

bauxite: a hydrated impure oxide of aluminium ($Al_2O_3 \bullet xH_2O$, with the amount of water x being variable). It is the main ore used to obtain aluminium metal. The reddish-brown colour of bauxite is mainly caused by the iron oxide impurities it contains.

beehive shelf: an inverted earthenware bowl with a hole in the upper surface and a slot in the rim. Traditionally, the earthenware was brown and looked similar to a beehive, hence its name. A delivery tube passes through the slot and a gas jar is placed over the hole. This provides a convenient way to collect gas over water in a pneumatic trough.

bell jar: a tall glass jar with an open bottom and a wide, stoppered neck that is used in conjunction with a beehive shelf and a pneumatic trough in some experiments involving gases. The name derives from historic versions of the apparatus, which resembled a bell in shape.

blast furnace: a tall furnace charged with a mixture of iron ore, coke and limestone and used for the refining of iron metal. The name comes from the strong blast of air introduced during smelting.

bleach: a substance that removes colour in stains on materials, either by oxidising or reducing the staining compound. *Example:* sulphur dioxide (SO_2).

block: one of the main divisions of the Periodic Table. Blocks are named for the outermost, occupied electron shell of an element. *Example:* The Transition Metals all belong to the d-block.

boiling point: the temperature at which a liquid boils, changing from a liquid to a gas. Boiling points change with atmospheric pressure. *Example:* The boiling point of pure water at standard atmospheric pressure is 100 °C.

boiling tube: A thin glass tube closed at one end and used for chemical tests, etc. The composition and thickness of the glass is such that it cannot sustain very high temperatures and is intended for heating liquids to boiling point. *See:* side-arm boiling tube, test tube.

bond: chemical bonding is either a transfer or sharing of electrons by two or more atoms. There are a number of types of chemical bond, some very strong (such as covalent and ionic bonds), others weak (such as hydrogen bonds). Chemical bonds form because the linked molecule is more stable than the unlinked atoms from which it formed. *Example:* the hydrogen molecule (H_2) is more stable than single atoms of hydrogen, which is why hydrogen gas is always found as molecules of two hydrogen atoms.

Boyle's Law: At constant temperature, and for a given mass of gas, the volume of the gas (V) is inversely proportional to pressure that builds up (P): $P \propto 1/V$.

brine: a solution of salt (sodium chloride, NaCl) in water.

Büchner flask: a thick-walled side-arm flask designed to withstand the changes in pressure that occur when the flask is connected to a suction pump.

Büchner funnel: a special design of plastic or ceramic funnel which has a flat stage on which a filter paper can be placed. It is intended for use under suction with a Büchner funnel.

buffer (solution): a mixture of substances in solution that resists a change in the acidity or alkalinity of the solution when small amounts of an acid or alkali are added.

burette: a long, graduated glass tube with a tap at one end. A burette is used vertically, with the tap lowermost. Its main use is as a reservoir for a chemical during titration.

burn: a combustion reaction in which a flame is produced. A flame occurs where *gases* combust and release heat and light. At least two gases are therefore required if there is to be a flame. *Example:* methane gas (CH_4) burns in oxygen gas (O_2) to produce carbon dioxide (CO_2) and water (H_2O) and give out heat and light.

calorimeter: an insulated container designed to prevent heat gain or loss with the environment and thus allow changes of temperature within reacting chemicals to be measured accurately. It is named after the old unit of heat, the calorie.

capillary: a very small diameter (glass) tube. Capillary tubing has a small enough diameter to allow surface tension effects to retain water within the tube.

capillary action: the tendency for a liquid to be sucked into small spaces, such as between objects and through narrow-pore tubes. The force to do this comes from surface tension.

carbohydrate: a compound containing only carbon, hydrogen and oxygen. Carbohydrates have the formula $C_n(H_2O)_n$, where n is variable. *Example:* glucose ($C_6H_{12}O_6$).

carbonate: a salt of carbonic acid. Carbonate ions have the chemical formula CO_3^{2-}. *Examples:* calcium nitrate $CaCO_3$ and sodium carbonate Na_2CO_3.

catalyst: a substance that speeds up a chemical reaction, but itself remains unaltered at the end of the reaction. *Example:* copper in the reaction of hydrochloric acid with zinc.

catalytic converter: a device incorporated into some exhaust systems. The catalytic converter contains a framework and/or granules with a very large surface area and coated with catalysts that convert the pollutant gases passing over them into harmless products.

cathode: the electrode at which reduction occurs; the positive terminal of a battery or the negative electrode of an electrolysis cell.

cathodic protection: the technique of protecting a metal object by connecting it to a more readily oxidisable metal. The metal object being protected is made into the cathode of a cell. *Example:* iron can be protected by coupling it with magnesium. Iron forms the cathode and magnesium the anode.

cation: a positively charged ion. *Examples:* calcium ion (Ca^{2+}), ammonium ion (NH_4^+).

caustic: a substance that can cause burns if it touches the skin. *Example:* Sodium hydroxide, caustic soda (NaOH).

Celsius scale (°C): a temperature scale on which the freezing point of water is at 0 degrees and the normal boiling point at standard atmospheric pressure is 100 degrees.

cell: a vessel containing two electrodes and an electrolyte that can act as an electrical conductor.

centrifuge: an instrument for spinning small samples very rapidly. The fast spin causes the components of a mixture that have a different density to separate. This has the same effect as filtration.

ceramic: a material based on clay minerals which has been heated so that it has chemically hardened.

chalcogens: the members of Group 6 of the Periodic Table: oxygen, sulphur, selenium and tellurium. The word comes from the Greek meaning 'brass giver', because all these elements are found in copper ores, and copper is the most important metal in making brass.

change of state: a change between two of the three states of matter, solid, liquid and gas. *Example:* when water evaporates it changes from a liquid to a gaseous state.

Charles's Law: The volume (V) of a given mass of gas at constant pressure is directly proportional to its absolute temperature (T): $V \propto T$.

chromatography: A separation technique uses the ability of surfaces to adsorb substances with different strengths. The substances with the least adherence to the surface move faster and leave behind those that adhere more strongly.

coagulation: a term describing the tendency of small particles to stick together in clumps.

coherent: meaning that a substance holds together or sticks together well, and without holes or other defects. *Example:* Aluminium appears unreactive because, as soon as new metal is exposed to air, it forms a very complete oxide coating, which then stops further reaction occurring.

coinage metals: the elements copper, silver and gold, used to make coins.

coke: a solid substance left after the gases have been extracted from coal.

colloid: a mixture of ultramicroscopic particles dispersed uniformly through a second substance to form a suspension which may be almost like a solution or may set to a jelly (gel). The word comes from the Greek for glue.

colorimeter: an instrument for measuring the light-absorbing power of a substance. The absorption gives an accurate indication of the concentration of some coloured solutions.

combustion: a reaction in which an element or compound is oxidised to release energy. Some combustion reactions are slow, such as the combustion of the sugar we eat to provide our energy. If the combustion results in a flame, it is called burning. A flame occurs where *gases* combust and release heat and light. At least two gases are therefore required if there is to be a flame. *Example:* the combustion or burning of methane gas (CH_4) in oxygen gas (O_2) produces carbon dioxide (CO_2) and water (H_2O) and gives out heat and light. Some combustion reactions produce light and heat but do not produce flames. *Example:* the combustion of carbon in oxygen produces an intense red–white light but no flame.

combustion spoon: also known as a deflagrating spoon, it consists of a long metal handle with a small cup at the end. Its purpose is to allow the safe introduction of a (usually heated) substance into a gas jar filled with gas, when the reaction is likely to be vigorous. *Example:* the introduction of a heated sodium pellet into a gas jar containing chlorine.

compound: a chemical consisting of two or more elements chemically bonded together. *Example:* Calcium atoms can combine with carbon atoms and oxygen atoms to make calcium carbonate ($CaCO_3$), a compound of all three atoms.

condensation: the formation of a liquid from a gas. This is a change of state, also called a phase change.

condensation nuclei: microscopic particles of dust, salt and other materials suspended in the air, that attract water molecules. The usual result is the formation of water droplets.

condensation polymer: a polymer formed by a chain of reactions in which a water molecule is eliminated as every link of the polymer is formed. *Examples:* polyesters, proteins, nylon.

conduction: (i) the exchange of heat (heat conduction) by contact with another object, or (ii) allowing the flow of electrons (electrical conduction).

conductivity: the ability of a substance to conduct. The conductivity of a solution depends on there being suitable free ions in the solution. A conducting solution is called an electrolyte. *Example:* dilute sulphuric acid.

convection: the exchange of heat energy with the surroundings produced by the flow of a fluid due to being heated or cooled.

corrosion: the oxidation of a metal. Corrosion is often regarded as unwanted and is more generally used to refer to the *slow* decay of a metal resulting from contact with gases and liquids in the environment. *Example:* Rust is the corrosion of iron.

corrosive: causing corrosion. *Example:* Sodium hydroxide (NaOH).

covalent bond: this is the most common form of strong chemical bonding and occurs when two atoms *share* electrons. *Example:* oxygen (O_2)

cracking: breaking down complex molecules into simpler compounds, as in oil refining.

crucible: a small bowl with a lip, made of heat-resistant white glazed ceramic. It is used for heating substances using a Bunsen flame.

crude oil: a chemical mixture of petroleum liquids. Crude oil forms the raw material for an oil refinery.

crystal: a substance that has grown freely so that it can develop external faces. Compare crystalline, where the atoms are not free to form individual crystals and amorphous, where the atoms are arranged irregularly.

crystalline: a solid in which the atoms, ions or molecules are organised into an orderly pattern without distinct crystal faces. *Examples:* copper(II) sulphate, sodium chloride. Compare amorphous.

crystallisation: the process in which a solute comes out of solution slowly and forms crystals. *See:* water of crystallisation.

crystal systems: seven patterns or systems into which all crystals can be grouped: cubic, hexagonal, rhombohedral, tetragonal, orthorhombic, monoclinic and triclinic.

cubic crystal system: groupings of crystals that look like cubes.

current: an electric current is produced by a flow of electrons through a conducting solid or ions through a conducting liquid. The rate of supply of this charge is measured in amperes (A).

decay (radioactive decay): the way that a radioactive element changes into another element due to loss of mass through radiation. *Example:* uranium 238 decays with the loss of an alpha particle to form thorium 234.

decomposition: the break down of a substance (for example, by heat or with the aid of a catalyst) into simpler components. In such a chemical reaction only one substance is involved. *Example:* hydrogen peroxide ($H_2O_2(aq)$) into oxygen ($O_2(g)$) and water ($H_2O(l)$).

decrepitation: when, as part of the decomposition of a substance, cracking sounds are also produced. *Example:* heating of lead nitrate ($Pb(NO_3)_2$).

dehydration: the removal of water from a substance by heating it, placing it in a dry atmosphere or using a drying (dehydrating) reagent such as concentrated sulphuric acid.

density: the mass per unit volume (e.g. g/cc).

desalinisation: the removal of all the salts from sea water, by reverse osmosis or heating the water and collecting the distillate. It is a very energy-intensive process.

desiccant: a substance that absorbs water vapour from the air. *Example:* silica gel.

desiccator: a glass bowl and lid containing a shelf. The apparatus is designed to store materials in dry air. A desiccant is placed below the shelf and the substance to be dried is placed on the shelf. The lid makes a gas-tight joint with the bowl.

destructive distillation: the heating of a material so that it decomposes entirely to release all of its volatile components. Destructive distillation is also known as pyrolysis.

detergent: a chemical based on petroleum that removes dirt.

Devarda's alloy: zinc with a trace of copper, which acts as a catalyst for reactions with the zinc.

diaphragm: a semipermeable membrane – a kind of ultrafine mesh filter – that allows only small ions to pass through. It is used in the electrolysis of brine.

diffusion: the slow mixing of one substance with another until the two substances are evenly mixed. Mixing occurs because of differences in concentration within the mixture. Diffusion works rapidly with gases, very slowly with liquids.

diffusion combustion: the form of combustion that occurs when two gases only begin to mix during ignition. As a result the flame is hollow and yellow in colour. *Example:* a candle flame.

dilute acid: an acid whose concentration has been reduced in a large proportion of water.

disinfectant: a chemical that kills bacteria and other microorganisms.

displacement reaction: a reaction that occurs because metals differ in their reactivity. If a more reactive metal is placed in a solution of a less reactive metal compound, a reaction occurs in which the more reactive metal displaces the metal ions in the solution. *Example:* when zinc metal is introduced into a solution of copper(II) sulphate (which thus contains copper ions), zinc goes into solution as zinc ions, while copper is displaced from the solution and forced to precipitate as metallic copper.

dissociate: to break bonds apart. In the case of acids, it means to break up, forming hydrogen ions. This is an example of ionisation. Strong acids dissociate completely. Weak acids are not completely ionised, and a solution of a weak acid has a relatively low concentration of hydrogen ions.

dissolve: to break down a substance in a solution without causing a reaction.

distillation: the process of separating mixtures by condensing the vapours through cooling.

distilled water: distilled water is nearly pure water and is produced by distillation of tap water. Distilled water is used in the laboratory in preference to tap water because the distillation process removes many of the impurities in tap water that may influence the chemical reactions for which the water is used.

Dreschel bottle: a tall bottle with a special stopper, designed to allow a gas to pass through a liquid. The stopper contains both inlet and outlet tubes. One tube extends below the surface of the liquid so that the gas has to pass through the liquid before it can escape to the outlet tube.

dropper funnel: a special funnel with a tap to allow the controlled release of a liquid. Also known as a dropping funnel or tap funnel.

drying agent: *See:* dehydrating agent.

dye: a coloured substance that will stick to another substance so that both appear coloured.

effervesce: to give off bubbles of gas.

effloresce: to lose water and turn to a fine powder on exposure to the air. *Example:* Sodium carbonate on the rim of a reagent bottle stopper.

electrical conductivity: *See:* conductivity

electrical potential: the energy produced by an electrochemical cell and measured by the voltage or electromotive force (emf). *See:* potential difference, electromotive force.

electrochemical cell: a cell consisting of two electrodes and an electrolyte. It can be set up to generate an electric current (usually known as a galvanic cell, an example of which is a battery), or an electric current can be passed through it to produce a chemical reaction (in which case it is called an electrolytic cell and can be used to refine metals or for electroplating).

electrochemical series: the arrangement of substances that are either oxidising or reducing agents in order of strength as a reagent, for example, with the strong oxidising agents at the top of the list and the strong reducing agents at the bottom.

electrode: a conductor that forms one terminal of a cell.

electrolysis: an electrical–chemical process that uses an electric current to cause the break-up of a compound and the movement of metal ions in a solution. The process happens in many natural situations (as for example in rusting) and is also commonly used in industry for purifying (refining) metals or for plating metal objects with a fine, even metal coating.

electrolyte: an ionic solution that conducts electricity.

electrolytic cell: *See:* electrochemical cell.

electromotive force (emf): the force set up in an electric circuit by a potential difference.

electron: a tiny, negatively charged particle that is part of an atom. The flow of electrons through a solid material such as a wire produces an electric current.

electron configuration: the pattern in which electrons are arranged in shells around the nucleus of an atom. *Example:* chlorine has the configuration 2, 8, 7.

electroplating: depositing a thin layer of a metal on to the surface of another substance using electrolysis.

element: a substance that cannot be decomposed into simpler substance by chemical means. *Examples:* calcium, iron, gold.

emulsion: tiny droplets of one substance dispersed in another. One common oil in water emulsion is called milk. Because the tiny droplets tend to come together, another stabilising substance is often needed. Soaps and detergents are such agents, wrapping the particles of grease and oil in a stable coat. Photographic film is an example of a solid emulsion.

endothermic reaction: a reaction that takes in heat. *Example:* when ammonium chloride is dissolved in water.

end point: the stage in a titration when the reaction between the titrant (added from a burette) and the titrate (in the flask) is complete. The end point is normally recognised by use of an indicator which has been added to the titrate. In an acid–base reaction this is also called the neutralisation point.

enzyme: biological catalysts in the form of proteins in the body that speed up chemical reactions. Every living cell contains hundreds of enzymes that help the processes of life continue.

ester: organic compounds formed by the reaction of an alcohol with an acid and which often have a fruity taste. *Example:* ethyl acetate ($CH_3COOC_2H_5$).

evaporation: the change of state of a liquid to a gas. Evaporation happens below the boiling point and is used as a method of separating the materials in a solution.

excess, to: if a reactant has been added to another reactant in excess, it has exceeded the amount required to complete the reaction.

exothermic reaction: a reaction that gives out substantial amounts of heat. *Example:* sucrose and concentrated sulphuric acid.

explosive: a substance which, when a shock is applied to it, decomposes very rapidly, releasing a very large amount of heat and creating a large volume of gases as a shock wave.

fats: semisolid, energy-rich compounds derived from plants or animals, made of carbon, hydrogen and oxygen. These are examples of esters.

ferment: to break down a substance by microorganisms in the absence of oxygen. *Example:* fermentation of sugar to ethanol during the production of alcoholic drinks.

filtrate: the liquid that has passed through a filter.

filtration: the separation of a liquid from a solid using a membrane with small holes (i.e. a filter paper).

flame: a mixture of gases undergoing burning. A solid or liquid must produce a gas before it can react with oxygen and burn with a flame.

flammable (also inflammable): able to burn (in air). *Opposite:* non-flammable.

flocculation: the grouping together of small particles in a suspension to form particles large enough to settle out as a precipitate. Flocculation is usually caused by the presence of a flocculating agent. *Example:* calcium ions are the flocculating agent for suspended clay particles.

fluid: able to flow; either a liquid or a gas.

fluorescent: a substance that gives out visible light when struck by invisible waves, such as ultraviolet rays.

flux: a material used to make it easier for a liquid to flow. A flux dissolves metal oxides and so prevents a metal from oxidising while being heated.

foam: a substance that is sufficiently gelatinous to be able to contain bubbles of gas. The gas bulks up the substance, making it behave as though it were semirigid.

fossil fuels: hydrocarbon compounds that have been formed from buried plant and animal remains. High pressures and temperatures lasting over millions of years are required. *Examples:* The fossil fuels are coal, oil and natural gas.

fraction: a group of similar components of a mixture. *Example:* In the petroleum industry the light fractions of crude oil are those with the smallest molecules, while the medium and heavy fractions have larger molecules.

fractional distillation: the separation of the components of a liquid mixture by heating them to their boiling points.

fractionating column: a glass column designed to allow different fractions to be separated when they boil. In industry, it may be called a fractionating tower.

free radical: a very reactive atom or group with a 'spare' electron. *Example:* methyl, $CH_3\bullet$.

freezing point: the temperature at which a substance undergoes a phase change from a liquid to a solid. It is the same temperature as the melting point.

fuel: a concentrated form of chemical energy. The main sources of fuels (called fossil fuels because they were formed by geological processes) are coal, crude oil and natural gas.

fuel rods: the rods of uranium or other radioactive material used as a fuel in nuclear power stations.

fume chamber or fume cupboard: a special laboratory chamber fitted with a protective glass shield and containing a powerful extraction fan to remove toxic fumes.

fuming: an unstable liquid that gives off a gas. Very concentrated acid solutions are often fuming solutions. *Example:* fuming nitric acid.

galvanising: applying a thin zinc coating to protect another metal.

gamma rays: waves of radiation produced as the nucleus of a radioactive element rearranges itself into a tighter cluster of protons and neutrons. Gamma rays carry enough energy to damage living cells.

gangue: the unwanted material in an ore.

gas/gaseous phase: a form of matter in which the molecules form no definite shape and are free to move about to uniformly fill any vessel they are put in. A gas can easily be compressed into a much smaller volume.

gas syringe: a glass syringe with a graduated cylinder designed to collect and measure small amounts of gases produced during an experiment.

gelatinous precipitate: a precipitate that has a jelly-like appearance. *Example:* iron (III) hydroxide. Because a gelatinous precipitate is mostly water, it is of a similar density to water and will float or lie suspended in the liquid. *See:* granular precipitate.

glass: a transparent silicate without any crystal growth. It has a glassy lustre and breaks with a curved fracture. Note that some minerals have all these features and are therefore natural glasses. Household glass is a synthetic silicate.

glucose: the most common of the natural sugars ($C_6H_{12}O_6$). It occurs as the polymer known as cellulose, the fibre in plants. Starch is also a form of glucose.

granular precipitate: a precipitate that has a grain-like appearance. *Example:* lead(II) hydroxide. *See:* gelatinous precipitate.

gravimetric analysis: a quantitative form of analysis in which the mass (weight) of the reactants and products is measured.

group: a vertical column in the Periodic Table. There are eight groups in the table. Their numbers correspond to the number of electrons in the outer shell of the atoms in the group. *Example:* Group 1: member, sodium.

Greenhouse Effect: an increase in the global air temperature as a result of heat released from burning fossil fuels being absorbed by carbon dioxide in the atmosphere.

Greenhouse gas: any of various the gases that contribute to the Greenhouse Effect. *Example:* carbon dioxide.

half-life: the time it takes for the radiation coming from a sample of a radioactive element to decrease by half.

halide: a salt of one of the halogens.

halogen: one of a group of elements including chlorine, bromine, iodine and fluorine in Group 7 of the Periodic Table.

heat: the energy that is transferred when a substance is at a different temperature to that of its surroundings. *See:* endothermic and exothermic reactions.

heat capacity: the ratio of the heat supplied to a substance, compared with the rise in temperature that is produced.

heat of combustion: the amount of heat given off by a mole of a substance during combustion. This heat is a property of the substance and is the same no matter what kind of combustion is involved. *Example:* heat of combustion of carbon is 94.05 kcal ($\times$ 4.18 = 393.1 kJ).

hydrate: a solid compound in crystalline form that contains water molecules. Hydrates commonly form when a solution of a soluble salt is evaporated. The water that forms part of a hydrate crystal is known as the 'water of crystallisation'. It can usually be removed by heating, leaving an anhydrous salt.

hydration: the process of absorption of water by a substance. In some cases hydration makes the substance change colour; in many other cases there is no colour change, simply a change in volume. *Example:* dark blue hydrated copper(II) sulphate ($CuSO_4 \bullet 5H_2O$) can be heated to produce white anhydrous copper(II) sulphate ($CuSO_4$).

hydride: a compound containing just hydrogen and another element, most often a metal.

Examples: water (H_2O), methane (CH_4) and phosphine (PH_3).

hydrous: hydrated with water. *See:* anhydrous.

hydrocarbon: a compound in which only hydrogen and carbon atoms are present. Most fuels are hydrocarbons, as is the simple plastic, polyethene. *Example:* methane CH_4.

hydrogen bond: a type of attractive force that holds one molecule to another. It is one of the weaker forms of intermolecular attractive force. *Example:* hydrogen bonds occur in water.

ignition temperature: the temperature at which a substance begins to burn.

immiscible: will not mix with another substance. e.g., oil and water.

incandescent: glowing or shining with heat. *Example:* tungsten filament in an incandescent light bulb.

incomplete combustion: combustion in which only some of the reactant or reactants combust, or the products are not those that would be obtained if all the reactions went to completion. It is uncommon for combustion to be complete and incomplete combustion is more frequent. *Example:* incomplete combustion of carbon in oxygen produces carbon monoxide and not carbon dioxide.

indicator (acid–base indicator): a substance or mixture of substances used to test the acidity or alkalinity of a substance. An indicator changes colour depending on the acidity of the solution being tested. Many indicators are complicated organic substances. Some indicators used in the laboratory include Universal Indicator, litmus, phenolphthalein, methyl orange and bromothymol. *See:* Universal Indicator.

induction period: the time taken for a reaction to reach ignition temperature. During this period, no apparent reaction occurs, then the materials appear to undergo spontaneous combustion.

inert: unreactive.

inhibitor: a substance that prevents a reaction from occurring.

inorganic substance: a substance that does not contain carbon and hydrogen. *Examples:* NaCl, $CaCO_3$.

insoluble: a substance that will not dissolve.

ion: an atom, or group of atoms, that has gained or lost one or more electrons and so developed an electrical charge. Ions behave differently from electrically neutral atoms and molecules. They can move in an electric field, and they can also bind strongly to solvent molecules such as water. Positively charged ions are called cations; negatively charged ions are called anions. Ions can carry an electrical current through solutions.

ionic bond: the form of bonding that occurs between two ions when the ions have opposite charges. *Example:* sodium cations bond with chloride anions to form common salt (NaCl) when a salty solution is evaporated. Ionic bonds are strong bonds except in the presence of a solvent. *See:* bond.

ionic compound: a compound that consists of ions. *Example:* NaCl.

ionise: to break up neutral molecules into oppositely charged ions or to convert atoms into ions by the loss of electrons.

ionisation: a process that creates ions.

isotope: an atom that has the same number of protons in its nucleus, but which has a different mass. *Example:* carbon 12 and carbon 14.

Kipp's apparatus: a piece of glassware consisting of three chambers, designed to provide a continuous and regulated production of gas by bringing the reactants into contact in a controlled way.

lanthanide series or lanthanide metals: a series of 15 similar metallic elements between lanthanum and lutetium. They are transition metals and also also called rare earths.

latent heat: the amount of heat that is absorbed or released during the process of changing state between gas, liquid or solid. For example, heat is absorbed when a substance melts and it is released again when the substance solidifies.

lattice: a regular arrangement of atoms, ions or molecules in a crystalline solid.

leaching: the extraction of a substance by percolating a solvent through a material. *Example:* when water flows through an ore, some of the heavy metals in it may be leached out causing environmental pollution.

Liebig condenser: a piece of glassware consisting of a sloping water-cooled tube. The design allows a volatile material to be condensed and collected.

liquefaction: to make something liquid.

liquid/liquid phase: a form of matter that has a fixed volume but no fixed shape.

lime (quicklime): calcium oxide (CaO). A white, caustic solid, manufactured by heating limestone and used for making mortar, fertiliser or bleach.

limewater: an aqueous solution of calcium hydroxide, used especially to detect the presence of carbon dioxide.

litmus: an indicator obtained from lichens. Used as a solution or impregnated into paper (litmus paper), which is dampened before use. Litmus turns red under acid conditions and purple in alkaline conditions. Litmus is a crude indicator when compared with Universal Indicator.

load (electronics): an impedance or circuit that receives or develops the output of a cell or other power supply.

lustre: the shininess of a substance.

malleable: able to be pressed or hammered into shape.

manometer: a device for measuring gas pressure. A simple manometer is made by partly filling a U-shaped rubber tube with water and connecting one end to the source of gas whose pressure is to be measured. The pressure is always relative to atmospheric pressure.

mass: the amount of matter in an object. In everyday use the word weight is often used (somewhat incorrectly) to mean mass.

matter: anything that has mass and takes up space.

melting point: the temperature at which a substance changes state from a solid phase to a liquid phase. It is the same as freezing point.

membrane: a thin, flexible sheet. A semipermeable membrane has microscopic holes of a size that will selectively allow some ions and molecules to pass through but hold others back. It thus acts as a kind of filter. *Example:* a membrane used for osmosis.

meniscus: the curved surface of a liquid that forms in a small bore or capillary tube. The meniscus is convex (bulges upwards) for mercury and is concave (sags downwards) for water.

metal: a class of elements that is a good conductor of electricity and heat, has a metallic lustre, is malleable and ductile, forms cations and has oxides that are bases. Metals are formed as cations

held together by a sea of electrons. A metal may also be an alloy of these elements. *Example:* sodium, calcium, gold. *See:* alloy, metalloid, non-metal.

metallic bonding: cations reside in a 'sea' of mobile electrons. It allows metals to be good conductors and means that they are not brittle. *See:* bonding.

metallic lustre: *See:* lustre.

metalloid: a class of elements intermediate in properties between metals and non-metals. Metalloids are also called semi-metals or semiconductors. *Example:* silicon, germanium, antimony. *See:* metal, non-metal, semiconductor.

micronutrient: an element that the body requires in small amounts. Another term is trace element.

mineral: a solid substance made of just one element or compound. *Example:* calcite is a mineral because it consists only of calcium carbonate; halite is a mineral because it contains only sodium chloride.

mineral acid: an acid that does not contain carbon and which attacks minerals. Hydrochloric, sulphuric and nitric acids are the main mineral acids.

miscible: capable of being mixed.

mixing combustion: the form of combustion that occurs when two gases thoroughly mix before they ignite and so produce almost complete combustion. *Example:* when a Bunsen flame is blue.

mixture: a material that can be separated into two or more substances using physical means. *Example:* a mixture of copper(II) sulphate and cadmium sulphide can be separated by filtration.

molar mass: the mass per mole of atoms of an element. It has the same value and uses the same units as atomic weight. *Example:* molar mass of chlorine is 35.45 g/mol. *See:* atomic weight.

mole: 1 mole is the amount of a substance which contains Avagadro's number (6×10^{23}) of particles. *Example:* 1 mole of carbon-12 weighs exactly 12 g.

molecular mass: *See:* molar mass.

molecular weight: *See:* molar mass.

molecule: a group of two or more atoms held together by chemical bonds. *Example:* O_2.

monoclinic system: a grouping of crystals that look like double-ended chisel blades.

monomer: a small molecule and building block for larger chain molecules or polymers ('mono' means one, 'mer' means part). *Examples:* tetrafluoroethene for teflon, ethene for polyethene.

native element: an element that occurs in an uncombined state. *Examples:* sulphur, gold.

native metal: a pure form of a metal, not combined as a compound. Native metal is more common in poorly reactive elements than in those that are very reactive. *Examples:* copper, gold.

net ionic reaction: the overall, or net, change that occurs in a reaction, seen in terms of ions.

neutralisation: the reaction of acids and bases to produce a salt and water. The reaction causes hydrogen from the acid and hydroxide from the base to be changed to water. *Example:* hydrochloric acid reacts with, and neutralises, sodium hydroxide to form the salt sodium chloride (common salt) and water. The term is more generally used for any reaction in which the pH changes toward 7.0, which is the pH of a neutral solution. *See:* pH.

neutralisation point: *See:* end point.

neutron: a particle inside the nucleus of an atom that is neutral and has no charge.

newton (N): the unit of force required to give one kilogram an acceleration of one metre per second every second (1 ms^{-2}).

nitrate: a compound that includes nitrogen and oxygen and contains more oxygen than a nitrite. Nitrate ions have the chemical formula NO_3^-. *Examples:* sodium nitrate $NaNO_3$ and lead nitrate $Pb(NO_3)_2$.

nitrite: a compound that includes nitrogen and oxygen and contains less oxygen than a nitrate. Nitrite ions have the chemical formula NO_2^-. *Example:* sodium nitrite $NaNO_2$.

noble gases: the members of Group 8 of the Periodic Table: helium, neon, argon, krypton, xenon, radon. These gases are almost entirely unreactive.

noble metals: silver, gold, platinum and mercury. These are the least reactive metals.

non-combustible: a substance that will not combust or burn. *Example:* carbon dioxide.

non-metal: a brittle substance that does not conduct electricity. *Examples:* sulphur, phosphorus, all gases. *See:* metal, metalloid.

normal salt: salts that do not contain a hydroxide (OH^-) ion, which would make them basic salts, or a hydrogen ion, which would make them acid salts. *Example:* sodium chloride (NaCl).

nucleus: the small, positively charged particle at the centre of an atom. The nucleus is responsible for most of the mass of an atom.

opaque: a substance that will not transmit light so that it is impossible to see through it. Most solids are opaque.

ore: a rock containing enough of a useful substance to make mining it worthwhile. *Example:* bauxite, aluminium ore.

organic acid: an acid containing carbon and hydrogen. *Example:* methanoic (formic) acid (HCOOH).

organic chemistry: the study of organic compounds.

organic compound (organic substance; organic material): a compound (or substance) that contains carbon and usually hydrogen. (The carbonates are usually excluded.) *Examples:* methane (CH_4), chloromethane (CH_3Cl), ethene (C_2H_4), ethanol (C_2H_5OH), ethanoic acid (C_2H_3OOH), etc.

organic solvent: an organic substance that will dissolve other substances. *Example:* carbon tetrachloride (CCl_4).

osmosis: a process whereby molecules of a liquid solvent move through a semipermeable membrane from a region of low concentration of a solute to a region with a high concentration of a solute.

oxidation–reduction reaction (redox reaction): reaction in which oxidation and reduction occurs; a reaction in which electrons are transferred. *Example:* copper and oxygen react to produce copper(II) oxide. The copper is oxidised, and oxygen is reduced.

oxidation: combination with oxygen or a reaction in which an atom, ion or molecule loses electrons to an oxidising agent. (Note that an oxidising agent does not have to contain oxygen.) The opposite of oxidation is reduction. *See:* reduction.

oxidation number (oxidation state): the effective charge on an atom in a compound. An increase in oxidation number corresponds to oxidation, and a decrease to reduction. Shown in Roman numerals. *Example:* manganate(IV).

oxidation state: *See:* oxidation number.

oxide: a compound that includes oxygen and one other element. *Example:* copper oxide (CuO).

oxidise: to combine with or gain oxygen or to react such that an atom, ion or molecule loses electrons to an oxidising agent.

oxidising agent: a substance that removes electrons from another substance being oxidised (and therefore is itself reduced) in a redox reaction. *Example:* chlorine (Cl_2).

ozone: a form of oxygen whose molecules contain three atoms of oxygen. Ozone is regarded as a beneficial gas when high in the atmosphere because it blocks ultraviolet rays. It is a harmful gas when breathed in, so low level ozone which is produced as part of city smog is regarded as a form of pollution. The ozone layer is the uppermost part of the stratosphere.

partial pressure: the pressure a gas in a mixture would exert if it alone occupied a flask. *Example:* oxygen makes up about a fifth of the atmosphere. Its partial pressure is therefore about a fifth of normal atmospheric pressure.

pascal: the unit of pressure, equal to one newton per square metre of surface. *See:* newton.

patina: a surface coating that develops on metals and protects them from further corrosion. *Example:* the green coating of copper carbonate that forms on copper statues.

percolate: to move slowly through the pores of a rock.

period: a row in the Periodic Table.

Periodic Table: a chart organising elements by atomic number and chemical properties into groups and periods.

pestle and mortar: a pestle is a ceramic rod with a rounded end, a mortar is a ceramic dish. Pestle and mortar are used together to pound or grind solids into fine powders.

Petri dish: a shallow glass or plastic dish with a lid.

petroleum: a natural mixture of a range of gases, liquids and solids derived from the decomposed remains of plants and animals.

pH: a measure of the hydrogen ion concentration in a liquid. Neutral is pH 7.0; numbers greater than this are alkaline; smaller numbers are acidic. *See:* neutralisation, acid, base.

pH meter: a device that accurately measures the pH of a solution. A pH meter is a voltmeter that measures the electric potential difference between two electrodes (which are attached to the meter through a probe) when they are submerged in a solution. The readings are shown on a dial or digital display.

phase: a particular state of matter. A substance may exist as a solid, liquid or gas and may change between these phases with addition or removal of energy. *Examples:* ice, liquid and vapour are the three phases of water. Ice undergoes a phase change to water when heat energy is added.

phosphor: any material that glows when energised by ultraviolet or electron beams, such as in fluorescent tubes and cathode ray tubes. Phosphors, such as phosphorus, emit light after the source of excitation is cut off. This is why they glow in the dark. By contrast, fluorescers, such as fluorite, only emit light while they are being excited by ultraviolet light or an electron beam.

photochemical smog: photochemical reactions are caused by the energy of sunlight. Photochemical smog is a mixture of tiny particles and a brown haze caused by the reaction of colourless nitric oxide from vehicle exhausts and oxygen of the air to form brown nitrogen dioxide.

photon: a parcel of light energy.

photosynthesis: the process by which plants use the energy of the Sun to make the compounds they need for life. In photosynthesis, six molecules of carbon dioxide from the air combine with six molecules of water, forming one molecule of glucose (sugar) and releasing six molecules of oxygen back into the atmosphere.

pipe-clay triangle: a device made from three small pieces of ceramic tube which are wired together in the shape of a triangle. Pipe-clay triangles are used to support round-bottomed dishes when they are heated in a Bunsen flame.

pipette: a log, slender, glass tube used, in conjunction with a pipette filler, to draw up and then transfer accurately measured amounts of liquid.

plastic: (material) a carbon-based substance consisting of long chains (polymers) of simple molecules. The word plastic is commonly restricted to synthetic polymers. *Examples:* polyvinyl chloride, nylon: **(property)** a material is plastic if it can be made to change shape easily. Plastic materials will remain in the new shape. (Compare with elastic, a property whereby a material goes back to its original shape.)

pneumatic trough: a shallow water-filled glass dish used to house a beehive shelf and a gas jar as part of the apparatus for collecting a gas over water.

polar solvent: a solvent in which the atoms have partial electric charges. *Example:* water.

polymer: a compound that is made of long chains by combining molecules (called monomers) as repeating units. ('Poly' means many, 'mer' means part.) *Examples:* polytetrafluoroethene or Teflon from tetrafluoroethene, Terylene from terephthalic acid and ethane-1,2-diol (ethylene glycol).

polymerisation: a chemical reaction in which large numbers of similar molecules arrange themselves into large molecules, usually long chains. This process usually happens when there is a suitable catalyst present. *Example:* ethene gas reacts to form polyethene in the presence of certain catalysts.

polymorphism: (meaning many shapes) the tendency of some materials to have more than one solid form. *Example:* carbon as diamond, graphite and buckminsterfullerene.

porous: a material containing many small holes or cracks. Quite often the pores are connected, and liquids, such as water or oil, can move through them.

potential difference: a measure of the work that must be done to move an electric charge from one point to the other in a circuit. Potential difference is measured in volts, V. *See:* electrical potential.

precious metal: silver, gold, platinum, iridium and palladium. Each is prized for its rarity.

precipitate: a solid substance formed as a result of a chemical reaction between two liquids or gases. *Example:* iron(III) hydroxide is precipitated when sodium hydroxide solution is added to iron(III) chloride. *See:* gelatinous precipitate, granular precipitate.

preservative: a substance that prevents the natural organic decay processes from occurring. Many substances can be used safely for this purpose, including sulphites and nitrogen gas.

pressure: the force per unit area measured in pascals. *See:* pascal, atmospheric pressure.

product: a substance produced by a chemical reaction. *Example:* when the reactants copper and oxygen react, they produce the product, copper oxide.

proton: a positively charged particle in the nucleus of an atom that balances out the charge of the surrounding electrons.

proton number: this is the modern expression for atomic number. *See:* atomic number.

purify: to remove all impurities from a mixture, perhaps by precipitation, or filtration.

pyrolysis: chemical decomposition brought about by heat. *Example:* decomposition of lead nitrate. *See:* destructive distillation.

pyrometallurgy: refining a metal from its ore using heat. A blast furnace or smelter is the main equipment used.

quantitative: measurement of the amounts of constituents of a substance, for example by mass or volume. *See:* gravimetric analysis, volumetric analysis.

radiation: the exchange of energy with the surroundings through the transmission of waves or particles of energy. Radiation is a form of energy transfer that can happen through space; no intervening medium is required (as would be the case for conduction and convection).

radical: an atom, molecule, or ion with at least one unpaired electron. *Example:* nitrogen monoxide (NO).

radioactive: emitting radiation or particles from the nucleus of its atoms.

radioactive decay: a change in a radioactive element due to loss of mass through radiation. For example, uranium decays (changes) to lead.

reactant: a starting material that takes part in, and undergoes, change during a chemical reaction. *Example:* hydrochloric acid and calcium carbonate are reactants; the reaction produces the products calcium chloride, carbon dioxide and water.

reaction: the recombination of two substances using parts of each substance to produce new substances. *Example:* the reactants sodium chloride and sulphuric acid react and recombine to form the products sodium sulphate, chlorine and water.

reactivity: the tendency of a substance to react with other substances. The term is most widely used in comparing the reactivity of metals. Metals are arranged in a reactivity series.

reactivity series: the series of metals organised in order of their reactivity, with the most reactive metals, such as sodium, at the top and the least react metals, such as gold, at the bottom. Hydrogen is usually included in the series for comparative purposes.

reagent: a commonly available substance (reactant) used to create a reaction. Reagents are the chemicals normally kept on chemistry laboratory benches. Many substances called reagents are most commonly used for test purposes.

redox reaction (oxidation–reduction reaction): a reaction that involves oxidation and reduction; a reactions in which electrons are transferred. *See:* oxidation–reduction.

reducing agent: a substance that gives electrons to another substance being reduced (and therefore itself being oxidised) in a redox reaction. *Example:* hydrogen sulphide (H_2S).

reduction: the removal of oxygen from, or the addition of hydrogen

to, a compound. Also a reaction in which an atom, ion or molecule gains electrons from an reducing agent. (The opposite of reduction is oxidation.)

reduction tube: a boiling tube with a small hole near the closed end. The tube is mounted horizontally, a sample is placed in the tube and a reducing gas, such as carbon monoxide, is passed through the tube. The oxidised gas escapes through the small hole.

refining: separating a mixture into the simpler substances of which it is made.

reflux distillation system: a form of distillation using a Liebig condenser placed vertically, so that all the vapours created during boiling are condensed back into the liquid, rather than escaping. In this way, the concentration of all the reactants remains constant.

relative atomic mass: in the past a measure of the mass of an atom on a scale relative to the mass of an atom of hydrogen, where hydrogen is 1. Nowadays a measure of the mass of an atom relative to the mass of one twelfth of an atom of carbon-12. If the relative atomic mass is given as a rounded figure, it is called an approximate relative atomic mass. *Examples*: chlorine 35, calcium 40, gold 197. *See:* atomic mass, atomic weight.

reversible reaction: a reaction in which the products can be transformed back into their original chemical form. *Example:* heated iron reacts with steam to produce iron oxide and hydrogen. If the hydrogen is passed over this heated oxide, it forms iron and steam. $3Fe + 4H_2O \rightleftharpoons Fe_3O_4 + 4H_2$.

roast: heating a substance for a long time at a high temperature, as in a furnace.

rust: the product of the corrosion of iron and steel in the presence of air and water.

salt: a compound, often involving a metal, that is the reaction product of an acid and a base, or of two elements. (Note 'salt' is also the common word for sodium chloride, common salt or table salt.) *Example:* sodium chloride (NaCl) and potassium sulphate (K_2SO_4) *See:* acid salt, basic salt, normal salt.

salt bridge: a permeable material soaked in a salt solution that allows ions to be transferred from one container to another. The salt solution remains unchanged during this transfer. *Example:* sodium sulphate used as a salt bridge in a galvanic cell.

saponification: a reaction between a fat and a base that produces a soap.

saturated: a state in which a liquid can hold no more of a substance. If any more of the substance is added, it will not dissolve.

saturated hydrocarbon: a hydrocarbon in which the carbon atoms are held with single bonds. *Example:* ethane (C_2H_6).

saturated solution: a solution that holds the maximum possible amount of dissolved material. When saturated, the rate of dissolving solid and that of recrystallisation solid are the same, and a condition of equilibrium is reached. The amount of material in solution varies with the temperature; cold solutions can hold less dissolved solid material than hot solutions. Gases are more soluble in cold liquids than in hot liquids.

sediment: material that settles out at the bottom of a liquid when it is still. A precipitate is one form of sediment.

semiconductor: a material of intermediate conductivity. Semiconductor devices often use silicon when they are made as part of diodes, transistors or integrated circuits. Elements intermediate between metals and non-metals

are also sometimes called semiconductors. *Example:* germanium oxide, germanium. *See:* metalloid.

semipermeable membrane: a thin material that acts as a fine sieve or filter, allowing small molecules to pass, but holding large molecules back.

separating column: used in chromatography. A tall glass tube containing a porous disc near the base and filled with a substance (for example, aluminium oxide, which is known as a stationary phase) that can adsorb materials on its surface. When a mixture is passed through the column, fractions are retarded by differing amounts, so that each fraction is washed through the column in sequence.

separating funnel: a pear-shaped, glassware funnel designed to permit the separation of immiscible liquids by simply pouring off the more dense liquid while leaving the less dense liquid in the funnel.

series circuit: an electrical circuit in which all of the components are joined end to end in a line.

shell: the term used to describe the imaginary ball-shaped surface outside the nucleus of an atom that would be formed by a set of electrons of similar energy. The outermost shell is known as the valence shell. *Example:* neon has shells containing 2 and 8 electrons.

side-arm boiling tube: a boiling tube with an integral glass pipe near its open end. The side arm is normally used for the entry or exit of a gas.

simple distillation: the distillation of a substance when only one volatile fraction is to be collected. Simple distillation uses a Liebig condenser arranged almost horizontally. When the liquid mixture is heated and vapours are produced, they enter the

condenser and then flow away from the flask and can be collected. *Example:* simple distillation of ethanoic acid.

slag: a mixture of substances that are waste products of a furnace. Most slags are composed mainly of silicates.

smelting: roasting a substance in order to extract the metal contained in it.

smog: a mixture of smoke and fog. The term is used to describe city fogs in which there is a large proportion of particulate matter (tiny pieces of carbon from exhausts) and also a high concentration of sulphur and nitrogen gases and probably ozone. *See:* photochemical smog.

smokeless fuel: a fuel which has been subjected to partial pyrolysis, such that there is no more loose particulate matter remaining. *Example:* Coke is a smokeless fuel.

solid/solid phase: a rigid form of matter which maintains its shape, whatever its container.

solubility: the maximum amount of a substance that can be contained in a solvent.

soluble: readily dissolvable in a solvent.

solute: a substance that has dissolved. *Example:* sodium chloride in water.

solution: a mixture of a liquid (the solvent) and at least one other substance of lesser abundance (the solute). Mixtures can be separated by physical means, for example, by evaporation and cooling. *See:* aqueous solution.

solvent: the main substance in a solution.

spectator ions: the ionic part of a compound that does not play an active part in a reaction. *Example:* when magnesium ribbon is placed in copper(II) sulphate solution, the copper is displaced from the solution by the magnesium, while the sulphate ion (SO_4^{2-}) plays no part in the reaction and so behaves as a spectator ion.

spectrum: a progressive series arranged using a characteristic etc. *Examples:* the range of colours that make up visible light (as seen in a rainbow) or across all electromagnetic radiation, arranged in progression according to their wavelength.

spontaneous combustion: the effect of a very reactive material or combination of reactants that suddenly reach their ignition temperature and begin to combust rapidly.

standard temperature and pressure (STP): 0°C at one atmosphere (a pressure which supports a column of mercury 760 mm high). Also given as 0°C at 100 kilopascals. *See:* atmospheric pressure.

state of matter: the physical form of matter. There are three states of matter: liquid, solid and gaseous.

stationary phase: a name given to a material which is used as a medium for separating a liquid mixture in chromatography.

strong acid: an acid that has completely dissociated (ionised) in water. Mineral acids are strong acids.

sublime/sublimation: the change of a substance from solid to gas, or vice versa, without going through a liquid phase. *Example:* iodine sublimes from a purple solid to a purple gas.

substance: a type of material, including mixtures.

sulphate: a compound that includes sulphur and oxygen and contains more oxygen than a sulphite. Sulphate ions have the chemical formula SO_4^{2-}. *Examples:* calcium sulphate $CaSO_4$ (the main

constituent of gypsum) and aluminium sulphate $Al_2(SO_4)_3$ (an alum).

sulphide: a sulphur compound that contains no oxygen. Sulphide ions have the chemical formula S^{2-}. *Example:* hydrogen sulphide (H_2S).

sulphite: a compound that includes sulphur and oxygen but contains less oxygen than a sulphate. Sulphite ions have the chemical formula SO_3^{2-}. *Example:* sodium sulphite Na_2SO_3.

supercooling: the ability of some substances to cool below their normal freezing point. *Example:* sodium thiosulphate.

supersaturated solution: a solution in which the amount of solute is greater than that which would normally be expected in a saturated solution. Most solids are more soluble in hot solutions than in cold. If a hot saturated solution is made up, the solution can be rapidly cooled down below its freezing point before it begins to solidify. This is a supersaturated solution.

surface tension: the force that operates on the surface of a liquid and which makes it act as though it were covered with an invisible, elastic film.

suspension: a mist of tiny particles in a liquid.

synthesis: a reaction in which a substance is formed from simpler reactants. *Example:* hydrogen gas and chlorine gas react to sythesise hydrogen chloride gas. The term can also be applied to polymerisation of organic compounds.

synthetic: does not occur naturally but has to be manufactured. Commonly used in the name 'synthetic fibre'.

tare: an allowance made for the weight of a container.

tarnish: a coating that develops as a result of the reaction between a metal and substances in the air. The most common form of tarnishing is a very thin, transparent oxide coating.

terminal: one of the electrodes of a battery.

test (chemical): a reagent or a procedure used to reveal the presence of another reagent. *Example:* litmus and other indicators are used to test the acidity or alkalinity of a substance.

test tube: A thin, glass tube, closed at one end and used for chemical tests, etc. The composition and thickness of the glass is such that, while it is inert to most chemical reactions, it may not sustain very high temperatures but can usually be heated in a Bunsen flame. *See:* boiling tube.

thermal decomposition: the breakdown of a substance using heat. *See* pyrolysis.

thermoplastic: a plastic that will soften and can be moulded repeatedly into shape on heating and will set into the moulded shape as it cools.

thermoset: a plastic that will set into a moulded shape as it cools, but which cannot be made soft by reheating.

thistle funnel: a narrow tube, expanded at the top into a thistlehead-shaped vessel. It is used as a funnel when introducing small amounts of liquid reactant. When fitted with a tap, it can be used to control the rate of entry of a reactant. *See:* burette.

titration: the analysis of the composition of a substance in a solution by measuring the volume of that solution (the titrant, normally in a burette) needed to react with a given volume of another solution (the titrate, normally placed in a flask). An indicator is often used to signal

change. *Example:* neutralisation of sodium hydroxide using hydrochloric acid in an acid–base titration. *See:* end point.

toxic: poisonous.

transition metals: the group of metals that belong to the d-block of the Periodic Table. Transition metals commonly have a number of differently coloured oxidation states. *Examples:* iron, vanadium.

Universal Indicator: a mixture of indicators commonly used in the laboratory because of its reliability. Used as a solution or impregnated into paper (Indicator paper), which is dampened before use. Universal Indicator changes colour from purple in a strongly alkaline solution through green when the solution is neutral to red in strongly acidic solutions. Universal Indicator is more accurate than litmus paper but less accurate than a pH meter.

unsaturated hydrocarbon: a hydrocarbon, in which at least one bond is a double or triple bond. Hydrogen atoms can be added to unsaturated compounds to form saturated compounds. *Example:* ethene, C_2H_4 or $CH_2=CH_2$.

vacuum: a container from which air has been removed using a pump.

valency: the number of bonds that an atom can form. *Examples:* calcium has a valency of 2 and bromine a valency of 1

valency shell: the outermost shell of an atom. *See:* shell.

vapour: the gaseous phase of a substance that is a liquid or a solid at that temperature. *Examples:* water vapour is the gaseous form of water, iodine vapour is the gaseous form of solid iodine. *See:* gas.

vein: a fissure in rock that has filled with ore or other mineral-bearing rock.

viscous: slow-moving, syrupy. A liquid that has a low viscosity is said to be mobile.

volatile: readily forms a gas.

volatile fraction: the part of a liquid mixture that will vaporise readily under the conditions prevailing during the reaction. *See:* fraction, vapour.

water of crystallisation: the water molecules absorbed into the crystalline structure as a liquid changes to a solid. *Example:* hydrated copper(II) sulphate $CuSO_4 \bullet 5H_2O$. *See:* hydrate.

weak acid and **weak base**: an acid or base that has only partly dissociated (ionised) in water. Most organic acids are weak acids. *See:* organic acid.

weight: the gravitational force on a substance. *See:* mass.

X-rays: a form of very short wave radiation.

MASTER INDEX